This book has been awarded
The Adèle Mellen Prize
for its distinguished contribution to scholarship.

Joan of Arc

Heretic, Mystic, Shaman

Anne Llewellyn Barstow

Studies in Women and Religion
Volume 17

The Edwin Mellen Press
Lewiston/Queenston/Lampeter

Library of Congress Cataloging-in-Publication Data

Barstow, Anne Llewellyn
 Joan of Arc : heretic, mystic, shaman

 (Studies in women and religion ; v. 17)
 Bibliography: p.
 Includes index.
 1. Joan of Arc, Saint, 1412-1431. 2. Christian
saints--France--Biography. 3. France--Religious life
and customs. 4. Feminism--Religious aspects--
Christianity. I. Title. II. Series.
 DC103.B28 1986   944'.026'0924 [B]   86-12756
 ISBN 0-88946-532-0 (alk. paper)

This is volume 17 in the continuing series
Studies in Women and Religion
Volume 17 ISBN 0-88946-532-0
SWR Series ISBN 0-88946-549-5

All rights reserved. For information contact:

The Edwin Mellen Press   The Edwin Mellen Press
Box 450   Box 67
Lewiston, New York   Queenston, Ontario
USA 14092   L0S 1L0 CANADA

The Edwin Mellen Press, Ltd.
Lampeter, Dyfed, Wales
UNITED KINGDOM SA48 7DY

Printed in the United States of America

To Alice Fetzer Carse,
Friend and colleague,
Who first introduced me to
Joan of Arc

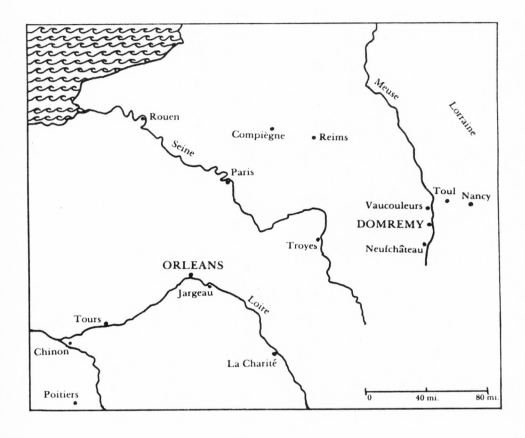

**THE FRANCE
OF JOAN OF ARC**

CONTENTS

ACKNOWLEDGEMENTS

The research and writing of this book were aided by a fellowship from the National Endowment for the Humanities and by a period of leave granted by the College at Old Westbury of the State University of New York.

I owe a debt of thanks to the following friends and colleagues who helped me talk through some of the problems I encountered: Karen Brown, Carol Duncan, Dana Greene, John Russell-Wood, Hilah Thomas, and the Feminist Scholars in Religion of New York; and for research to Susannah Driver, Miriam Ross, and the Inter-Library loan staff at the College of Old Westbury.

I am grateful to the late Joan Kelly, whose encouragement over the years was a support and whose work on women's history and on Christine de Pisan in particular is a model for us all.

Tom F. Driver gave me both comments and practical assistance throughout the writing of the book, maintaining an interest in Joan of Arc that encouraged me in my own pursuit of Joan's voice for today. His comments as theologian complemented my own as historian, and I am grateful for his contribution to this project.

A.L.B.

INTRODUCTION

In studying women's roles in religious history I search for women who have acted autonomously, who, despite the overwhelming influence of men on Christianity and Judaism, have made an authentic witness as women. I listen for the voice which comes out of female experience, which speaks on its own authority. Given my interest in autonomous female spirituality, I am surprised that I waited so long to turn to Joan of Arc. One of the most independent women in history and one of the few medieval women to make a political impact, Joan claimed two different sources of power, the supernatural authority of mysticism and an uncompromising radical individualism. Speaking for herself in every instance, she relied on neither priests nor family nor military allies; she stood alone, her only defense her belief in her own truth.

Joan has been much written about in French patriotic historiography[1] and in Catholic apologetics,[2] but not by feminist scholarship. Two obstacles to a feminist approach to Joan, her mystical experiences and her role as a military leader, may have discouraged feminist historians. There is the further point that she was burned at the stake, and feminists have not been looking for martyrs. Of her death, so problematic for feminists, I will not speak again until the last chapter.

---

1. Among a number of studies of Joan as savior of France, two old ones are especially valuable: Jules Michelet, *Joan of Arc*, trans. Albert Guérard (Paris, 1853; Ann Arbor: University of Michigan Press, 1957), which is taken from Michelet's vast *Histoire de France*, vol. 5 (1841); and Pierre Champion, *Procès de condemnation de Jeanne d'Arc*, 2 vols. (Paris, 1920-1921), partially trans. in W.P. Barrett; see below, n. 6.

2. Works celebrating Joan as a Christian saint and martyr: Charles Péguy's drama, *The Mystery of the Charity of Joan of Arc* (Paris, 1912; trans. Julian Green, New York: Pantheon Books, 1950); Paul Claudel's oratorio, *Jeanne au Bûcher*, set to music by Honegger, text in *Théatre*, ed. J. Madaule (Paris, 1965); Paul Doncoeur, *Le mystère de la passion de Jeanne d'Arc* (Paris: A l'Art Catholique, 1929); Jean Guitton, *Problème et mystère de Jeanne d'Arc* (Paris: Favard, 1961); and E. Delaruelle, *La spiritualité de Jeanne d'Arc* (Toulouse, 1964).

That Joan's famous moments occurred in the world of men requires comment at the outset; indeed, that she carried out her mission as a military leader in the arena of war might indicate that she was a male-identified woman. But when we reflect that any person living in France in the latter days of the Hundred Years' War would have been caught up in its tragic events, we can better understand Joan's commitment to a military solution to her country's crisis. She had other options, as we shall see; Joan might have served her country in ways other than on the battlefield. Her commitment to the army, therefore, was an authentic part of her character which cannot be ignored. Recalling further that in Joan's time, as in our own, there was virtually no public sphere for women, no place for a prophetically gifted woman to act except in centers of male power, then we must accept Joan's attraction to the man's world of court and army.

The more difficult problem for a feminist scholar, however, is that the central experience of Joan's life was her voices. A heroine who bases the direction of her life on paranormal visions, who defends the truth of her divinely-inspired messages until death, is not easily understood by the present-day women's movement. In our day, persons who hear voices are considered mad. And yet it is not only inadvisable, it is futile to study Joan without considering what she maintained was the central experience of her life.[3]

***

This book is not a biography of Joan; there are many reliable accounts of her life available, a new one appearing almost every year.[4] I offer instead a study of the topics most revealing of how Joan lived as an autonomous woman in fifteenth-century France. Because Joan's central experience was visionary, one must look at the

---

3. Consider for example the perceptive but flawed study by Marina Warner, *Joan of Arc: The Image of Female Heroism* (New York: Alfred A. Knopf, 1981). Warner's study is imaginative but lacks sufficient knowledge of two subjects essential to understanding Joan, the inquisition and medieval mysticism. See my review of Warner's book in *American Historical Review* (April, 1982):437-438, and my Chapter Two, no. 5, below.

4. Of the many biographies available, one might begin with the recent study by Frances Gies, *Joan of Arc: the Legend and the Reality* (New York: Harper & Row, 1981). Particularly sympathetic to the role of Joan's voices is the biography by Andrew Lang, *The Maid of France* (London: Longmans, 1909). An excellent introduction both to Joan's life and to the primary sources is Régine Pernoud, *Joan of Arc, by Herself and her Witnesses*, trans. Edward Hyams (New York: Stein & Day, 1966), in which Joan and her contemporaries speak through their recorded words.

tradition of late medieval mysticism; since her defense of her visions led her into what the church considered to be heresy, we must consider the history of medieval dissent. In her role as heroine of the French resistance, Joan was perceived as a magic worker; to understand her charismatic qualities we must turn to the literature of shamanism. Given that the church labelled her magical powers as witchcraft, we must study how belief in diabolism was developing in her century. Finally, we will consider why the roles of shaman and of mystic were especially useful to women in Joan's time. Before exploring how an understanding of late medieval popular religion and its mystical tradition are essential to an understanding of Joan, I offer the reader a brief summary of the events of her life and of the political situation upon which she made her mark.

Born into a peasant family in the village of Domremy,[5] where the eastern border of France met the duchy of Lorraine, Joan did not know her exact age, but the year of her birth was most likely 1412. Since Domremy did not have a school, Joan's education lacked book learning. She learned instead from her mother Isabelle Romée, whose spiritual seeking had taken her on pilgrimage. Joan reported that although she "did not know A from B," still she had been taught her prayers (the Pater and Ave Maria) and the art of spinning by her mother. Beyond that, there was local lore, a rich accumulation of oral wisdom available to Joan from her numerous godmothers. Joan remembered that some of these women had told her the legends of the local Fairy Tree and healing fountain, and as we shall see, Joan took part in many of the traditional customs, both Christian and pre-Christian.

In the century before her birth France had been invaded many times by the English, and during Joan's childhood the English scored one of their greatest victories, the destruction of the French army at Agincourt, capping that with a diplomatic triumph, their alliance with the French duchy of Burgundy. When her neighborhood was overrun by Burgundian soldiers in 1428, Joan and her family were

---

5. That Joan's father was a tenant farmer and one of the spokesmen for the village in time of crisis has been taken by some historians to mean that Joan was not a peasant (for example, Malcolm Vale, *Charles VII*, p. 46). There is ample evidence however that the d'Arc family were little different from any village family in their poverty ("they were very poor," a neighbor reported at the retrial), level of education, or other resources, facts which place them squarely in the peasant class. That the peasantry was in a better position than it had been for centuries, due to the demand for its labor created by the bubonic plague, is true enough; the d'Arc family, as peasants, were members of a rising class (George Holmes, *Europe: Hierarchy and Revolt, 1320-1450, pp. 249-250*).

forced to flee to a nearby walled town.

When she was about thirteen, Joan began to hear voices. Given the desperate military crisis in her land, it is not surprising that the voices told her of "the great misery that was in France;" more remarkable is that they instructed this illiterate peasant girl to go to the Dauphin, Charles, the uncrowned king, to help him drive the English out of France. For four or five years she did not act, although the voices did not cease to admonish her. Telling no one of her extraordinary visitations but nonetheless arranging her life in order to receive them, she refused marriage with a young man of her village, vowed her virginity to her voices (whom she later identified as two female saints and an archangel), and spent as much time in prayer as possible.

When the last French stronghold north of the Loire, Orléans, was beseigned in 1428, Joan could remain passive no longer. Convincing a cousin of her mission, she used him to get away from home and to reach the nearby French garrison at Vaucouleurs. Converting others there to her vision, she acquired male clothing, a sword, a horse, and armed escorts to accompany her to the Dauphin. Winning over Charles, his astrologer, his theologians, and some of his court, Joan was permitted to lead the Armagnac army in lifting the siege of Orléans. Her image as young maid in armor, combined with her successful prophecies, telepathic knowledge, and ability to speak with angels, so fired up the dispirited army that they turned the tide of war. Capturing several more towns and receiving the allegiance of a number of others, Joan and the army were able to escort the Dauphin to Rheims where he was crowned as Charles VII, in July, 1429.

Joan's winning streak was soon over. After several defeats and a winter of inactivity, she was captured by Burgundians at Compiègne. Sold to the English, who turned her over to French theologians loyal to the English cause, Joan was put on trial, not as a prisoner of war but as a heretic. Her testimony as she defended the authenticity of her voices is not only valuable evidence about mystical experience but is also a witness to individual conscience, rare in any time, audacious for a young peasant woman challenged by a powerful priesthood.

In May, 1431, Joan was condemned as a heretic and a witch and was burned at the stake.

***

Both by the solitary nature of her visionary experience and by ecclesiastical condemnation, Joan was an outsider. In order to locate outsiders, usually one must move beyond the normal range of historical inquiry. It is not only that their ecstatic experiences are difficult for the modern mind, scholarly or otherwise, to grasp. The problem is compounded by the fact that they seldom move in the circles of power, and that their stories are recorded most often by their enemies. As we read Joan's words we must remember that they were written down by officials hostile to her. But because Joan was active in ruling circles, and because inquisitional courts kept records, we have extensive if biased evidence for both her thoughts and actions.

Our chief documentation for Joan's life is the trial record, and the evidence gathered at the retrial which took place intermittently from 1450 to 1456;[6] the retrial cleared Joan's name of heresy, without dealing with the main issue on which she had been condemned, namely, her right to claim authority for her divine messengers. In addition, there is brief mention of Joan in several chronicles of the time, and in several contemporary literary works, most important of which are the Bourgeois of Paris' memoir, Christine de Pisan's poem and Jean Gerson's essay in defense of Joan.[7]

6. I will refer primarily to the English translation of the trial and retrial by T. Douglas Murray, *Jeanne d'Arc, Maid of Orleans* (New York: McClure, Phillips & Co., 1902), supplemented by material in the translation of W.P. Barrett, *Trial of Jeanne d'Arc, with an essay by Pierre Champion* (London: Gotham House, 1932), in W.S. Scott's translation of the Orléans manuscript, *Trial of Joan of Arc* (London: The Folio Society, 1956), and in Régine Pernoud's edition of the retrial, *Retrial of Joan of Arc*, trans. J.M. Cohen (London: Methuen, 1955). The best French edition of the trial is Pierre Tisset and Yvonne Lanhers, *Procès de condamnation de Jeanne d'Arc*, newly annotated (Paris: Klincksieck, 1960), and of the retrial, P. Doncoeur and Y. Lanhers, *La réhabilitation de Jeanne la Pucelle* and further volumes (Paris, 1956-1961); *Le procès en nullité de la condamnation de Jeanne d'Arc*, ed. Pierre Duparc (Paris, 1977). The best collection of materials on Joan remains the five volumes published by Jules Quicherat, *Procès de condamnation et de réhabilitation de Jeanne d'Arc dite la Pucelle d'Orléans* (Paris: Renouard, 1841-1849; New York: Johnson Reprint Corp., 1965), the first volume of which is the Latin text of the trial.

7. The chronicle accounts are unsatisfactory, being utterly contradictory, offering little concrete detail about Joan, and reflecting the opinions of their various patrons; see Charles W. Lightbody's critical discussion of the fifteenth-century chronicle accounts in *The Judgments of Joan: A Study in Cultural History* (London: Allen and Unwin, 1961), chaps. 2-3. More useful works contemporary with Joan's life are the Bourgeois of Paris, *A Parisian Journal, 1405-1449*, trans. J. Shirley (Oxford, 1968); Christine de Pisan, *Ditié de Jeanne d'Arc*, ed. and trans. Angus J. Kennedy and Kenneth Varty (Oxford: Society for the Study of Medieval Languages and Literature, 1977); Jean Gerson, "De quadam Puella," in Dorothy G. Wayman, "The Chancellor and Jeanne d'Arc," *Franciscan Studies* 17.2-3 (June-Sept., 1957):273-305, translated in the Appendix below.

To understand Joan, however, requires one to go beyond these sources; one must also come to terms with the mystical tradition of the late middle ages. Trained as a social historian, I had considered mystical experience too subjective, too narrowly individualistic, to be utilized in historical study. Worse, I was convinced that mystics were narcissists, claiming special relationship with the divine, and escapists, other-worldly types who turned their backs on problems that less favored mortals were left to struggle with. While a moment's reflection would have shown me that Joan did not fit the latter stereotype, nonetheless I lumped her in with the others called mystics.

I did not develop an interest in mysticism until I was forced to, while hearing adulatory, uncritical papers on Catherine of Siena, Theresa of Avila, Thérèse of Lisieux, and Julian of Norwich–three nuns who were made saints and a classic lay mystic. Given the strongly individual nature of the mystical experience, I asked how these four famous mystics all happened to hear messages that were acceptable to the church. True, Theresa encountered opposition to her work, but she achieved sainthood quickly. My education in mysticism began with the realization that they were "good girls," women whose revelations told them what their confessors and bishops wanted to hear. Were there no "bad girl" mystics? No one who heard what the church would not approve? As I began to recall spiritually gifted women who had run into trouble with church authorities–Mechtild of Magdeburg, Prous Boneta, Marguerite Porete, Anne Hutchinson–I was at once struck by two facts that had previously escaped me: these women were all critics of their churches, courageous in defending their own truth–and they all got into serious trouble for it. I knew then where to look for the mystics who would interest me: in the records of the inquisition. There I found evidence of mystics who reached the state of illumination without male guidance and persevered in living out their mission without male support. I take this as proof of autonomous female spiritual experience.

It is the mystical vision as a mandate for autonomous action that concerns me. Consider the uses of revelation that go against the grain: Mechtild of Magdeburg judging the popes of her time by her illuminations and finding that they deserved to die,[8] Anne Hutchinson challenging the Puritan authorities at the direct insistence of God,[9] Somalian wives challenging their husbands' domi-

8. Mechtild of Magdeburg, *The Flowing Light of the Godhead*, trans. L. Menzies (London, 1953), p. 189.
9. Francis J. Bremer, ed. *Anne Hutchinson: Troubler of the Puritan Zion* (Huntington:

nance through the commands of a medium,[10] Haitian devotees who, when possessed, demand jobs through the spirits who possess them.[11] Just as mysticism is manifested in all religions, so it is put to subversive use by its practitioners in many different cultures. I seek the mystic who is a religious agitator, whose vision the authorities will not tolerate.

Given this subversive possibility inherent in mystical experience, it is not surprising that women, denied the usual means of influence in public life, have turned to mysticism as a path to influence, as a way of having a voice in affairs otherwise closed to them. Mystical expression is especially crucial in finding one's voice, in turning inward, turning away from male teachers and authorities, from male literature and man-made laws.

Only then can women be autonomous, only by developing consciousness, as they do today, or by turning inward to find their voice, as Joan and other medieval women did. Because this experience is the key to autonomous thought and action, I therefore had to deal with mysticism. But for my purposes I had to be selective. Reflecting on the way the church co-opted the messages of Theresa of Avila and Thérèse of Lisieux, I realized that, for my uses, the mystics who achieve sainthood are suspect. Can those whose messages found favor with persons in power have explored the depth of their own truth? Elmer O'Brien maintains that authentic mystical experience must go against what the receiver has known or believed, must create a struggle within the subject and, by implication, may create a conflict between the subjects and their society.[12] I have turned to those who had to defend their truth, even to the point of death. It is the controversial mystics who best throw light on their society, on what it tolerates or brands as criminal or demonic, on what leverage it allows to the individual, on what it expects of women or rejects as dangerous. While saints confirm the society's ideals, either actualized or theorized, heretical mystics show up both what their world valued and what it condemned.

Joan's own age found her to be heterodox. Condemned by her church as a witch and heretic, she is not to be connected with the sainthood bestowed upon her five hundred years later. The canoni-

Krieger Publishing Co., 1981).

10. I.M. Lewis, *Ecstatic Religion: An Anthropological Study of Spirit Possession and Shamanism* (Baltimore: Penguin Books, 1971), pp. 70-79.

11. Alfred Mètraux, *Voodoo in Haiti*, trans. Hugo Charteris (New York: Schocken Books, 1972), pp. 95-96.

12. Elmer O'Brien, *Varieties of Mystic Experience* (London: Mentor-Omega Books, 1973).

zation proceedings in the early twentieth century were a political accommodation to the French Right; they did not touch on the issues on which Joan had been condemned–the authority and authenticity of her voices–and therefore left the question of the value of her witness unclear.

It is heretic Joan, not Saint Joan, who can teach us more about the state of spiritual life in fifteenth-century France. And it is for that reason that we must learn what we can about religion as it was practised by ordinary people in Joan's lifetime.

Popular religion, by definition the religion of the majority, was the focus of spiritual life for that seventy percent of the European population who were rural villagers. Although it was the religion of the majority, it was not the religion of the powerful.

I.M. Lewis has pointed out that:

> mystical experience, like any other experience, is grounded in and must relate to the social environment in which it is achieved. It thus inevitably bears the stamp of the culture and society in which it arises.[13]

Popular religion drew its practitioners from the periphery of power, and through its use of vision and magic provided religious expression to those classes and that gender who were denied access to the influence enjoyed by the ruling class. It was therefore the vehicle–the *only* vehicle in late medieval society–through which a young girl of the peasant class could gain a voice, could achieve visibility. Because it was Joan of Arc's religion, we will begin with an exploration of the resources it offered.

BRIEF CHRONOLOGY

1403	The Dauphin born (future king Charles VII of France).

Joan's Early Life

1412 ?	Joan of Arc born at Domremy in Lorraine.
1415	Battle of Agincourt (major victory of English over French).
1420	Treaty of Troyes (Dauphin Charles rejected: thrones of both France and England will belong to the English king).
1425 ?	Joan begins hearing voices.
1428	Joan flees with her family to Neufchâteau, to escape marauding English-Burgundian troops.

Joan's Mission: Victories

1429

Jan.	Joan goes to Vaucouleurs to seek an escort to the Dauphin.
Feb./Mar.	Reaches the Dauphin's court at Chinon.
Mar.	Examined by the Dauphin's theologians at Poitiers.
Apr. 24	Begins career with the Armagnac army.
Apr. 28 to May 8	Battle of Orléans; **the siege is raised.**

| June | Capture of Jargeau, Meung, and Patay. |

| July 5 | At Troyes; meets Brother Richard. |

| July 17 | Coronation of Charles VII at Rheims. |

| Nov. 2 | Capture of St. Pierre-le-Moutier. |

Joan's Mission: Defeats
1429

| Aug. to Sep. | Charles VII signs truce with Burgundians and withdraws to Gion. |

| Sep. 8 | Joan fails to capture Paris. |

| Nov. | Meets Catherine de la Rochelle. |

| Nov. | Fails to capture La Charité-sur-Loire. |

| Dec. 25 | With Br. Richard and Pieronne at Jargeau. |

1430

| May 23 | Captured by Burgundians at Compiègne. |

| Nov. | Sold to the English, who turn her over to the French Bp. Cauchon to be tried for heresy. |

Joan's Trial at Rouen, 1431

| Feb. 21 - May 23 | Examined and condemned by her judges. |

| May 19 | Condemned by the University of Paris. |

| May 24 | Recants. |

| May 27 | Withdraws her recantation. |

| May 30 | Burned at the stake. |

Aftermath
1436

| | King Charles reclaims Paris. |

1450	English driven out of Normandy.
1450-1456	Joan's posthumous retrial.
1456	The 1431 verdict nullified.
1869	Canonization proceedings begun.
1920	Joan becomes a saint.

Joan of Arc

Heretic, Mystic, Shaman

Chapter One
Late Medieval Popular Religion

Not far from Domremy there is a tree that they call "The Ladies' Tree"–others call it "The Fairies' Tree;" nearby there is a spring where people sick of the fever come to drink....I have sometimes been [there] to play with the young girls...I may have danced there formerly.
Joan of Arc, the Trial, February, 1431

One fact must be considered at the beginning, one piece of context that goes far toward making Joan's life understandable: she lived within a spiritual milieu quite different from the religions with which we are familiar, different not only from most of twentieth-century Christianity but also from the Christianity of the establishment of her own day.

Call it popular, or folk, or traditional religion, it was the religion of the majority of Europeans until at least 1700. Highly syncretistic, it utilized some of the forms of elite Christianity but modified them to accord with its own needs and understandings. Mixing elements of folk culture, including pre-Christian legends and practices, with the forms of classical Christianity, the European masses created in effect their own religion.

Although none exists, a magisterial study of European folk religion is badly needed.[1] While there is general agreement, for example, that the religious beliefs and practices of the elite and of the masses were vastly different, there is little that can be said without contradiction about the implications of that fact. One cannot find consensus even on the over-all contours of these two aspects of religion: Peter Brown, for example, considers that Europe had achieved a Christianized society by the end of the sixth century, whereas both Robert Muchembled and Jean Delumeau conclude that

---

1. Natalie Zemon Davis, "Some Tasks and Themes in the Study of Popular Religion," in *The Pursuit of Holiness*, ed. Charles Trinkhaus and Heiko Oberman (Leiden: Brill, 1974), pp. 307-325. Davis warns that lay piety must not be judged by the standards of the theologians, that "laymen and lay women were sometimes active, indeed innovative, in sacred matters...," pp. 308-309.

the Christianizing of the rural areas was still being carried out in the seventeenth.[2]

Given such widely differing opinions from reliable historians, one must of course ask about their definitions. Who makes up society? The ruling class converted sooner, and used Christian institutional structures to help them govern. What part of Europe is studied? Religion in the north, for example, retained much of its pagan character for centuries longer than in the south, and in both areas urban episcopal centers struggled to control and convert pagan countryside. Finally, what are the criteria for a Christian society? In referring to a culture that consisted of a small minority of Christian elite ruling a semi-pagan peasantry, one speaks of "a Christian society" only by ignoring seventy percent of the population. Given this problem, in describing the conditions of Joan's time, I will draw whenever possible on materials from peasant culture in the northern French lands of the fifteenth-century, and their traditional roots.

Because historians are lured by the published sources of elite religion, we have neglected the more recalcitrant evidences of popular religion, but they are there. Collections of European folklore and the recent increase in studies of popular culture, parish sermons, heretical beliefs, lay piety, and witchcraft, all provide fruitful material for reconstructing the religion of medieval Europe. Further knowledge can be found in an unsuspected direction: the folk religion of pre-1700's Europe bears considerable resemblance to the traditional religions still practised in many parts of the world. The work of anthropologists and scholars of comparative religions can therefore fill in a number of blanks after other historical materials have been exhausted.

The following sketch of pre-modern European religion is drawn from these composite sources. Positing that the popular religion of Europe was far more than a mere reaction to elite Christianity, I agree with Peter Brown that it is not to be viewed as "a diminution, a misconception, or a contamination of 'unpopular religion.'"[3] Certainly it cannot be reduced to "superstition." I will argue that the

2. Peter Brown, "Sorcery, Demons, and the Rise of Christianity: from Late Antiquity to the Middle Ages," *Religion and Society in the Age of St. Augustine*, ed. Peter Brown (London: Faber & Faber, 1972). Robert Muchembled, "The Witches of the Cambrésis: The Acculturation of the Rural World in the Sixteenth and Seventeenth Centuries," *Religion and the People: 800-1700*, ed. James Obelkevich (Chapel Hill: University of North Carolina Press, 1978), pp. 221-276. Hereafter, "Cambrésis." Jean Delumeau, *Le Catholicisme entre Luther et Voltaire* (Paris: Nouvelle Clio, 1971).

3. Peter Brown, "Sorcery, Demons...," p. 232. The cities were more aware of Christian moral values and theology than the countryside.

religion of the populace had deep roots in pre-Christian religions, in Joan's area specifically in Celtic practices, and that from this rich past it maintained its own ethical and theological integrity.

One should think, in this context, of a religion of villages, of rural life. While the movement of villagers into towns, a process continuous in Western Europe from the eleventh century, brought their country-side religion into the urban areas, steadily injecting peasant "paganism" into hierarchical Christianity, still popular religion must be thought of primarily as bearing a rural stamp.[4] Because almost all of its practitioners were illiterate, it was a religion of oral traditions with beliefs passed on within families and by the wiser members of the community. It was above all a religion of individualism, that is, of each person's relationship to the spirits. A villager might rely on the aid of a wise woman for advice from the spirits about when to plant crops or how to keep a lover, but ultimately the answer depended on the state of that individual's relationship with certain spirits.

In this sense, the religion was based on reciprocity. One bargained with the spirits; one expected much from them, much that was concrete and particular, and one had to be prepared to give in return. The spirits, who in many cases became the Christian saints, were not thought of as totally "other" than human beings; they had once been, in this life, after all, outstanding local persons or even family members.

We may think of a balance between the powers of the two worlds, based on a sense of unity or reciprocity between them, a belief in mutual communication and trade-offs. Because it served in place of Christian belief and sacramental practice, the custom of calling on the spirits was suspect in the eyes of Christian officialdom, who challenged the identity of the spirits and labelled the petitioning of them as ignorant and anti-sacramental.

As most of its devotees were farmers or herders, the popular religion was nature-centered. Trees, springs, rocks, and other objects in nature were sacred. Hill-tops were especially numinous, and many promontories boasted shrines to mark miraculous events that went back to pre-Christian times. Because parts of nature, places, and persons connected with those places were believed to have supernatural power, they were considered to be enspirited and sometimes became spirits or quasi-deities. That a huge, ancient tree, a healing

4. Peter Brown, *The Cult of the Saints: Its Rise and Function in Latin Christianity* (Chicago: University of Chicago Press, 1981), p. 19; Brown's discussion of the need to attend to popular religion runs from pp. 12-22.

spring, and a hill-top shrine all played a part in Joan of Arc's early religious experience is not surprising, for similar spirit-charged sites, with rituals and customs attendant upon them, were to be found in, or more often outside of, every village of Europe. Fulfilling many functions–social, agricultural, and divinatory–they served two primary needs of the European peasantry: healing and match-making.

By praying at a holy place, one might be instructed through a vision as to how to heal oneself: an herbal cure for a stomach ache, or a poultice of warm wax for dropsy or ear ache.[5] The sacred waters of a well might restore sight to blind eyes or mobility to para-lyzed limbs. When illness struck, medieval people turned to all avail-able sources of healing: doctors (who were often clerics), Christian saints and shrines, and village mid-wives and wise women, with their amulets, herbs, and advice about efficacious actions or propitiations of angry spirits. The sick, while willing to cover all bases, probably turned first to their nearest aid, the village diviner.

There was little alternative to such traditional cures, blood-letting and purging being the stock in trade of university-trained doctors as well as village charmers. Yet the church knew that the source of the healers' powers was not Christian, lying rather in innate qualities, inherent capacities stemming from a mysterious personal *mana*, and it therefore felt compelled to accuse the healers of magic and witch-craft. Because of this, a lay person performed cures at some risk. Despite harassment, however, folk medicine retained immense popu-larity. Evidence comes, for example, from *Piers Plowman*, where a character who had first tried Christian doctors finally found relief from a long illness in being treated by two witches, an old cobbler-woman and one "Dame Emma."[6] A leading thirteenth-century alche-mist, Michael Scot, recommended that when doctors fail, the sick should not refuse to go to "diviners and enchantresses, although this may seem wrong."[7]

Folk medicine remained useful well into the modern period and is even today enjoying a revival. Keith Thomas explained its hold on both the European peasantry then and third-world peoples today when he wrote that

5. Many examples of healing are listed by Ronald C. Finucane in chap. 4 of his *Miracles and Pilgrims: Popular Beliefs in Medieval England* (Totowa, New Jersey: Rowman and Littlefield, 1977). While his study concentrates on miracles at Christian shrines, Finucane points out that to draw a distinction between folk healing and offi-cially sanctioned Christian miracles is inappropriate; see 62ff.

6. Finucane, *Miracles and Pilgrims*, p. 69.

7. Ibid. Finucane draws on Lynn Thorndike's study, *Michael Scot*, p. 78.

They cherish the dramatic side of healing, the ritual acting out of sickness, and the symbolic treatment of disease in its social context. Primitive psychotherapy, in particular, can compare favorably with its modern rivals....

Thomas touches on a role that Joan of Arc briefly played when he concludes that

In the light of modern research into the medical role of faith and imagination it seems that [the village healer's] claim to effect healing by touch, by command, by incantation, or even by action at a distance, must be taken seriously.[8]

The celebration of sexuality, that human need for which Christianity provided no outlet, was perhaps the activity for which village Europe most needed its old religious customs. Under 'fairy trees' and in great oak woods across the continent, rural Europeans carried out courtship and practiced adultery, often utilizing their non-Christian holidays and agricultural festivals for this purpose. Dancing, drinking, pairing off, villagers made the most of warm summer nights in order to escape from their homes, where they often had no privacy, out into the woodlands. The church had good reason to be suspicious of these festivals: involving sexual license, they were a celebration of the "rites of spring."

In England lively May Games were presided over by a May King and Queen. Villagers, including children, went to the woods where "they spend all the night in pleasant pastimes," and from there they brought back birch-boughs and a maypole; the maypole games often ended in sexual play, the winner being paired off with the Queen of May. The Spanish celebrated May Day with mock weddings, in which a little boy and a little girl were placed on a marriage bed. The focus on trees, poles, and boughs was inherited from Druidic customs, and the entire spring celebration of dancing, love-making, and healing came from ancient Celtic rites;[9] like Celtic religion, these folk practices were intensely local and always polytheistic.

This immediate, materialistic form of the sacred led to the importance of the human body as an icon. The power of certain holy bodies was stronger in the minds of many than the doctrine of salva-

8. Keith Thomas, *Religion and the Decline of Magic* (New York: Scribners, 1971), pp. 207, 210.

9. Peter Burke, *Popular Culture in Early Modern Europe* (New York: Harper & Row, 1978), p. 194 and n. 37.

tion offered by the church. Illness was healed by the touch of a hand, a curse was laid by an evil eye. Pieces of hair, nail clippings, even the dirt from a holy man's body and the water in which he washed, contained miraculous power. This cult of the body reached its extreme form in the high middle ages, with reports of stigmata, levitations, and return to life from near-death.[10]

Focus on the sacredness of special bodies was at the heart of the cult of the saints: the frenzied traffic in relics, in which saints' bones were sold and re-sold, were fabricated and even stolen, developed out of people's belief in the miraculous power of holy bodies. While the gospels give ample evidence of the use of magic in early Christianity, the new religion did not at first have a cult of saints. Peter Brown has shown how this changed when a belief in the power of "the very special dead" swept across the Latin Church in the fourth century; but Brown considers this to have been the experience primarily of the urban aristocrats.[11]

To the contrary, Patrick Geary, utilizing material from Carolingian times, has argued that the common people in the eighth and ninth centuries had a cult of holy persons, a continuation of their pre-Christian cults under the color of new Christian labels. The commoners' ancient belief in the magical powers of holy persons either was transferred to the saints offered them by the Roman church or, in the majority of cases, remained focused on a local hero or heroine. Geary's research indicates, *contra* Brown, that the European masses had a cult of magical persons long before Christianity began to make inroads. When the local cult could not be dislodged, the church finally adopted it, incorporating the pagan patron, however awkwardly, into its own burgeoning pantheon. Geary concludes that European peasant culture continued this practice into early modern times.[12] To Christian theologians this was seen as paganism.

10. Norman Cohn, *The Pursuit of the Millennium* (New York: Harper Torchbooks, 1961), pp. 36, 79; Finucane, *Miracles and Pilgrims*, pp. 73-75.

11. Peter Brown, *The Cult of the Saints.* On the use of magic in primitive Christianity, see Morton Smith, *Jesus the Magician* (New York: Harper & Row, 1976).

12. Patrick J. Geary, "The Ninth-Century Relic Trade: A Response to Popular Piety?" in *Religion and the People*, ed. Obelkevich, pp. 8-19. "In many essential aspects, the Carolingian effort to give a specifically Roman focus to the cult of holy men in the empire was a failure. European peasant culture demonstrated a remarkable ability to adapt elements of this form of elite religion without sacrificing what would continue to be, in many ways, a separate culture. So-called pagan or rustic forms of individual and group devotion to saints continued throughout the Middle Ages and beyond...the great majority of popular saints in the later Middle Ages would be either local saints or saints in some way associated with local traditions."

Folk religion was based on the principle of magic. Because rural people expected to bargain with God and fully believed that such practice would be efficacious, they were consoled by magic. Fear and social unrest were dealt with by recourse to exorcists, and the use of magic charms, spells, amulets, and especially the ability of the magic worker to see into and advise about the future, gave medieval people a certain control over the forces in their lives.[13] Village life was more stable and coherent than we tend to realize; since in popular religion, the sacred penetrated everywhere and was available to almost everyone at all times, people had a cushion against both violence and despair. The old religion's understanding of evil was a help: when one can blame someone else (the witch) or some other force (demonic magic) for all misfortune, including death, then one need not struggle with much self-doubt, guilt, or unfocused anger.

Perhaps this accommodating aspect of magic, its ability to work for one or against one's enemies, accounts for the remarkable flexibility of social relationships in medieval village life. Of course ill feeling and even violence sometimes broke out, but by and large the communities functioned without coercive peace-keeping from outside. Robert Muchembled maintains that kinship ties restrained hatreds and regulated the solving of conflicts, and the society appeared willing "to hear the complaints of all its citizens." With all its problems, the medieval village stopped short of violence that would destroy it.[14] But whereas the uses of magic were not seen by these masses as anti-Christian but were utilized freely for both benevolent and malevolent purposes, the Christian elite labelled these beliefs and practices as superstitious and, what was worse, as witchcraft.

Folk religion was preeminently based on individual experience. The necessity for negotiating with God and with his spirits tended to make the divine available to each person, to make individuals responsible for their own ultimate spiritual welfare. The belief was generally held that "God breaks out all over," that the Holy Spirit moves

13. Muchembled, "Cambrésis," pp. 269-270.

14. Ibid. Karen Brown remarks on a similar capacity among present-day Haitian practioners of vodoun, whose language "creates the distance that allows for separate selves to co-exist without devouring each other. A person must always be left free to misunderstand." Brown, "The Vévé of Haitian Vodou: A Structural Analysis of Religious Imagery," unpubl. dss., Temple University, 1976: pp. 69-70. This "grey area" mentality is very different from the thought of the Western elite, with its either/or dichotomies. I suggest that there were two basic modes of discourse in the medieval world, the philosophically-based language of the elite and the situation-defined language of the masses. When the two were forced into dialogue, the result could be brutal; Joan of Arc's trial stands as a prime example.

where it will, that any person might be visited by, or might call on, divine powers. This fact kept popular religion open to continuing revelation and gave it a changing, dynamic, spontaneous quality. More important for our study, it assured that popular religion would maintain an egalitarian nature. Because the Holy Spirit might speak through anyone, the authority figures in popular religion might come from any group or class, from the lowest ranks of the peasantry, or even from women or children.

In the earlier middle ages holy people most often became famous by performing magical acts. In the fourteenth and fifteenth centuries, however, a new type of spiritually gifted person became popular, the seer. Known today as "the mystics," such persons made their name by producing prophecies, sometimes uncannily accurate, in other cases merely astonishing in their boldness or eccentricity. So useful were these holy prognosticators that not only ordinary people but kings and popes sought them out. Although these visionaries often lived in a cemetery or near the tomb of a miracle-worker,[15] the source of their power was not a magical act; it was their vision of, or direct communication with, a spirit or with God. Joan of Arc had this type of visionary experience, without accompanying signs. The message she received was sign enough for her, even though her contemporaries pressed her for a sign visible to them.

Often the mystics' message was a private one, concerned only with the salvation of one person or possibly a few other individual souls. But when the communication related the mystic to a group of people, involving her in the destiny of a community or even of a nation, as did Joan's "voice," and when it forced her into the role of prophet or catalyst or inspired leader of that group, then the mystic moved beyond the role of individual *inspirée* to that of shaman. I use the term to mean the mediumistic leader, the one who crosses the barrier into the spirit world in order to bring back the knowledge necessary to save the people from peril, *and who then becomes the one who leads*, who takes them out of danger, away from destruction. This role takes the shaman beyond the mystic, whose visionary advice may have been crucial but who merely pointed the way for others to act.

15. The Bourgeois of Paris reported that in Paris in 1442 the recluse Jeanne la Verrière was installed by the bishop of Paris "in a little brand new dwelling place in the Innocents' graveyard." He preached the installation sermon before a large crowd; *A Parisian Journal: 1404-1449*, trans. Janet Shirley (Oxford: Oxford University Press, 1968), p. 348 and n. Hermits were popular for the way they symbolized extreme asceticism, a true dying to this world. In chap. 3 we will meet Marie Robine, another holy inhabitant of a cemetery, whose visions were believed to foretell Joan of Arc's mission.

In using the term "shaman" I am not, of course, referring to the possessed priesthood of the classic shamanistic regions of the Arctic and South America, whose bodies are possessed by spirits and who go on long "spirit journeys" into the heavens or below the earth.[16] Anthropologists utilize the word "shaman," however, in many areas of the world today–India, the South Pacific, Korea, Japan, Africa, and more–for former societies such as ancient Greece, and for many functions other than those strictly associated with the Siberian and Amazonian shamans. The characteristics that I am concerned with begin by a sudden, spontaneous call from the spirit world, often at puberty, that is traumatic and causes conflict and even illness. Both males and females are claimed in this way, men more often by the spirits of powerful, "central" religious organizations, women more often by the spirits of marginal or protest groups. Male shamans typically preside over established cults that maintain the moral standards of a group, females are called on to control outside threats from foreign sources of evil, being turned to more often in times of group crisis, as Joan was. But both sexes are drawn frequently from deprived groups and appear at times when their community suffers desperate affliction and deprivation.

The person receiving this call withdraws from society in order better to receive spirit messages; she spends time alone, preferably in remote retreats in nature. She is hounded by her spirits, until finally *she* gains control of *them*. Then she has a breakthrough, an illumination, and often literally sees a powerful light. She receives a new identity, with different clothing, a new name, and a new relationship to her fellow-humans. She now belongs sexually to her spirits and must modify or break off sexual relations with others. She gains gifts of prophecy and healing.

But the shaman must be acknowledged by her group as having these powers, as being the conduit to the secret knowledge of the gods. Much of her power, therefore, is incarnate in her role. The crisis in her community may force her to a showdown with enemy leaders; the enemy may be the priests of a rival or a non-charismatic

16. This description of shamanism is based on I.M. Lewis, *Ecstatic Religion: An Anthropological Study of Spirit Possession and Shamanism*, chaps. 2, 3, 6. However, I side with Mircea Eliade, *Shamanism: Archaic Techniques of Ecstasy*, trans. W.R. Trask (Princeton: Bollingen Foundation/Princeton University Press, 1964) against the latter's argument that all shamans experience spirit possession. See Lewis, pp. 49-51. I regret that John A. Grim's study, *The Shaman: Patterns of Siberian and Ojibway Healing* (Norman: University of Oklahoma Press, 1983) appeared too late to be used here. His descriptions of the transforming power of the shamanic vision quest, and of how Ojibway women improve their status through spirit contact, are germane.

sect. The shaman both envisions *and enacts* the role of salvific leader; to be more specific, the shaman takes known roles or types and plays into them. The title, the role, the particular spirit, god, or whatever, is part of the social lore. The charismatic leader casts herself in the role, and, so to speak, "makes it come true." And in the end...but there are two possible endings. In the "good" myth, the shaman presides over the victory sacrifice; in the tragic myth, the shaman herself is the sacrifice, the propitiation for the failure of her group.

The dynamic, spontaneous quality of folk religion, with its sudden, unexpected call, enabled it to be the source both of new popular enthusiasms and of revolts against established power, whether ecclesiastical or secular. Finding the social, as well as the religious, dynamic of folk religion impossible to control, the Christian establishment labelled it heresy and lived in horror of it.

***

The roots of popular religion in medieval France and certain other parts of Europe appear to lie in Celtic religion. At the time that the Romans conquered the region where Joan later grew up, the term "Celtic" best identified the culture of the people living there.[17] Complete as was Caesar's military conquest, the Romans in no way obliterated the culture or religion of the long-established tribes of the Vosges, nor, for that matter, of most of the peoples of north-central Europe.[18] Roman paganism established a great temple to Apollo at Grand, eighteen kilometers from Domremy, and the usual martyrs to the young Christian faith duly appeared in the neighborhood, whereas the establishment of Christianity as the Roman state religion in the fourth century brought a bishopric to the area, at Toul.[19] But the religious practices of the people of the Vosges continued virtually unchanged, even being reinforced in the late sixth and seventh centuries by the arrival of Celtic **missionaries** from Ireland. Now Christian, these Irish monks were nonetheless representatives of a Celtic culture that had not been Romanized: Ireland itself was never conquered, never even invaded by Rome, and the Irish Church developed its own distinctive forms of

17. The following description of Celtic religion is based on the accounts of Barry Cunliffe, *The Celtic World* (New York: McGraw-Hill, 1979), and Gerhard Herm, *The Celts: The People Who Came out of the Darkness* (New York: St. Martin's Press, 1976), chaps. 8, 9 and 15.

18. Cunliffe, pp. 156-158.

19. Pierre Marot, *Joan the Good Lorrainer at Domremy* (Colmar: Editions S.A.E.P., 1981), pp. 5-6.

Christianity, sometimes in opposition to the Church of Rome.

When the Irish monk Columban entered France in 590, he "swept through the country like a whirlwind: he hurled crockery at the feet of the Merovingian king because his court was so un-Christian in its ways; peasants said to each other that he even terrified bears in the forest." Called a "sturdy berserker of Christianity," in the memorable phrase of the historian Arno Borst, Columban sounds much like a possessed, shamanic master of the animals, yet he achieved solid results as a Christian missionary in Joan's area, founding the long-lasting monastic communities of Luxeuil and Fontaine.[20] Other Irish monks founded Remiremont nearby, and there were many other Celtic outposts, stretching across northern Europe from the mouth of the Seine to Vienna. To the Frankish lands they brought a special gift, the Archangel Michael, a powerful warrior spirit from Mediterranean lands on whom the Irish had bestowed some of their favorite magical characteristics.[21]

For Celtic peoples, the spirits were everywhere. In springs and at the sources of rivers, in special animals such as bulls, in large trees, sacred groves, and oddly-shaped rocks, the Celts met their gods. While they did build temples, their sacred places were usually found in nature. Seeing "no frontier between the human and the infernal,"[22] they sought frequent communion with their gods. Dreading excommunication as the worst of punishments, they believed that one "has to be in communion with the gods through the medium of sacrifice and offering,"[23] that one must placate the gods. Because the Celtic religious sense was strongly marked by the principle of reciprocity, the Celts filled their sacred pools and shafts with gifts for the gods.[24]

They had a rich and varied pantheon to turn to. A chief male god represented each tribe, balanced by a Great Queen with whom he mated on either August 1 or November 1, the two great harvest festivals. While this couple fulfilled the fertility rites for each Celtic "nation," a few gods achieved trans-tribal reknown: Lug, poet and magician who won battles with the help of magic,[25] a serpent god of healing, female gods of healing, a mother goddess of healing named Bridget who after the Celts' conversion made her way into Christian sainthood, a patroness of horses named Epona,[26] and a woodland

20. Herm, p. 269. He gives no location for the words quoted from Borst.
21. Ibid., p. 265.
22. Ibid., p. 154.
23. Cunliffe, p. 90.
24. Ibid.
25. Herm, p. 155.

spirit who commanded the animals.[27] Believing in strength in
numbers, the Celts often portrayed a god three times, or with two or
three faces, a trinity.[28]

Some Celtic practices are traceable as far back as six-thousand
years into the European past, a reminder of the remarkable continuity of religious traditions.[29] The scholar of shamanism, Mircea
Eliade, believes that the Celtic priesthood may have been influenced
by shamanistic practices learned from Scythian invaders from the
Asian steppes where the priesthood was shamanic.[30] Since we know
that Europeans took over a number of important Scythian customs–
improved horsemanship, a new style of jewelry-making, individual
burial, an aristocratic class structure, head-hunting, and very likely a
belief in life after death[31] –we can assume that they also adopted
some characteristics of the Scythian shamans.

Since communication with and propitiation of the gods was of the
first importance, Celts gave great power to those who could summon
and 'appease the spirits. Their priesthood, both male and female, was
made up of two orders: druids, persons of great knowledge who
were the teachers, judges, medical specialists, astronomers, diplomats, peace-makers, and guardians of the traditions of the Celtic
world; and seers of augurers, whose skill at sacrificing enabled them
to be intermediaries between the tribe and the gods, to insure the
well-being of the community, and to foretell the future.[32]

The seers were shamanistic magicians, so trusted by the Celts that
they were authorized to preside over the ultimate ritual of human
sacrifice. When a murder had been committed, atonement must be
observed; when rain or victory in battle was essential to survival, the
gods must be conciliated; sometimes animals would suffice, but the
highest offerings were the burned bodies of human beings. Burnt
sacrifices were offered by enclosing live humans in wicker cages and
setting fire to them.[33] The seers were charismatic leaders, experi-

26. Ibid., pp. 159, 265.

27. Cunliffe, p. 76.

28. Ibid., p. 69.

29. Ibid., p. 97. Perhaps their most ancient deity was the horned god. Portraits of
this patron of hunting, adorned with antlers, are found on neolithic cave walls, and he
was surely first a human priest. With this figure of the shaman we are close to the
origins of religion. As another example of the conservatism of religious practices, on
p. 94 Cunliffe describes two Celtic shrines with identical features built seven hundred
years apart (c. 900 B.C.E. - 200 B.C.E.).

30. Mircea Eliade, *Shamanism*, as referred to by Herm, pp. 153-154.

31. Herm, pp. 105-108.

32. Cunliffe, pp. 106-108.

encing possession and leading warriors into ecstatic trance before battle. Herm gives us a dramatic picture of Celtic priests:

> They took part in mysteries that may seem sinister to us, leading a people that saw no frontier between the human and the infernal, practised ecstatic rites, self-abasement, orgies, blood-sacrifices, made head-hunting sacred out of religious conviction and indeed possessed the shamanistic traits that centuries-old reports ascribe to them. Their gods were just as they were themselves.[34]

Perhaps the Celts' most deeply held religious belief was their belief in the soul. This conviction sustained their hope in life after death and led to their most exotic custom, the cult of the human head. Believing that the soul resided in the head, they reasoned that in order to control a person and to gain his power for oneself, one must possess his head. Gathering skulls both from slain enemies and from dead family members, they decorated their homes and temples with these grisly charms and even wore them as amulets. Preserving them carefully in chests,[35] in a manner exactly reminiscent of Scythian practice, they cleaned out the skulls, gilded the interior, and used them as liturgical drinking vessels in temple ritual.[36]

The ritual use of skulls, so foreign to classical Christian usage, appears to have made a lasting impression on the people of Lorraine. In 1982 in the Roman Catholic cathedral of Toul, I observed four skulls, the crania of a woman, a layman, and two bishops of Toul, including the first bishop, St. Mansuy, enthroned in 365. Carefully exhibited in gilded chests, these ancient skulls are not in a museum but rather are placed in the transept of the church at the entrance to the choir, a place of honor for a prized reliquary. While I do not know what the Christians of Toul today think of this shrine, I know that to me it is proof sufficient of the continuity of religious traditions.

***

---

33. Ibid., p. 69.

34. Herm, pp. 154-155. They also communicated with the gods by ritual cannibalism, that is, they sometimes led the people in eating the limbs of persons who had been sacrificed. On cannibalism, see Cunliffe, p. 108.

35. Cunliffe, pp. 82-83.

36. On the Scythian cult of the head, Herm, p. 105; on the Celtic cult, Herm, pp. 152-153.

Throughout the middle ages and well into modern times, rural religion, by maintaining its dependence on local magic and on inspired visionaries of both sexes, remained a channel for new, individual religious expression. In contrast to what Robert Muchembled has called this "dynamic, receptive, not yet congealed" type of cult enriched by its "magical milieu,"[37] official Christianity was defined by intellectual categories, especially dogma and canon law; it was channelled into well-defined liturgy; and it confined its leadership almost entirely to its male priesthood. Over the centuries it became more suspicious of individual revelation, of any contact with the divine not mediated through its priesthood, and as its internal tensions increased in the late medieval period, its tolerance of the charismatic individual grew thin.

The Roman Church had been wracked with internal problems since the beginning of the fourteenth century. Surviving its "captivity" by the French monarchy beginning in 1303, and the papacy's long exile in the French city of Avignon from 1307 to 1376, it was stunned in mid-century by the devastations of bubonic plague which killed perhaps as many as one-third of its personnel. This "Black Death" injured the church in more than this one way: as the single largest landholder in Europe, the church felt painfully the drop in landlords' incomes that followed the epidemic, and perhaps even more important, its prestige for miracle-working suffered badly when Europeans learned that the sacraments could do nothing to protect them from the plague.

The church's magic found wanting, people turned more to their own resources. And as the church struggled with this insubordination, in the decades just preceding Joan's mission it met the difficult challenge of internal political chaos.[38] The simultaneous election of two popes in 1378, creating the Great Schism, greatly reduced the already flagging prestige of the papacy and pushed the papal government inexorably in the direction it did not want to take: toward conciliar government, a dangerous form of power-sharing.

---

37. Robert Muchembled, "Witchcraft, Popular Culture, and Christianity in the Sixteenth Century with Emphasis upon Flanders and Artois," trans. Patricia M. Ranum, in *Ritual, Religion, and the Sacred: Selections from the "Annales,"* vol. 7, ed. Robert Forster and Orest Ranum (Baltimore: Johns Hopkins University Press, 1982), pp. 230, 214. Hereafter referred to as Muchembled, "Witchcraft."

38. Excellent descriptions of these events can be followed in E. Delaruelle, et al., *L'église au temps du Grand Schisme et de la crise conciliare, 1378-1449* (Paris: Bloud et Gay, 1964) and *History of the Church*, eds. Hubert Jedin and John Dolan, trans. Anselm Biggs (New York: Crossroad Publishing Co. 1970), vol. 4, chap. 46.

The great legislative and theological work of the thirteenth century had provided the Roman church with a superb base; the challenge of the late medieval period was whether the church could use this power and this unsurpassed ability to define the faith and yet remain responsive to European society. The over-all result of the fourteenth- and fifteenth-century crises, however, was to make the church more rigid, more dogmatic, one might say paranoid. This hardening may be noticed in three respects: a continuing but grudging accommodation to certain aspects of popular religion (which the church called paganism); outright refusal to accommodate certain deviant groups (which it labelled heretical); and finally, at the end of the medieval period, a violent reaction to what the church saw as the remaining superstitions, now grouped together into a heretical conspiracy against Christian society that it called witchcraft.

In the intermixing of the two religions, elite and popular, it is well known that the folk form syncretized heavily with the classic form of Christianity. What is less often acknowledged is the extent to which elite Christianity and its practitioners were influenced by the popular expression. Christianity, for example, had always had its own share of magic: Jesus was remembered as a powerful miracle worker, and the early church, basing its highest claims on the bodily resurrection, soon added to that the miracle of a virgin birth. The height of Christian magic was approached in the twelfth century, however, by the doctrine of transubstantiation. Theological formulations and popular mentality alike thought of the Eucharistic host as transformed into the flesh of Christ through a priestly act of supernatural power.

The earliest saints were venerated more for their powerful magic than for their moral example: St. Martin of Tours, for instance, made the sign of the cross to stop a pagan funeral procession and to save himself from a falling tree. He claimed the sign of the cross would protect him in battle; he repeated the word *crux* ("Cross") as a magical chant; and it was said that his breath was enough to exorcise a demon.[39] Many converts to Christianity from Celtic or other religions made the change because they assumed they were gaining access to a superior source of magic, to a new and more powerful form of miracle-working. Similar reasons were observed by early missionaries in Africa: the aspect of Christianity which many Africans first identified with or responded to were Biblical stories of powerful magical

39. Aline Rousselle, "From Sanctuary to Miracle-Worker: Healing in Fourth-Century Gaul," *Ritual, Religion, and the Sacred*, eds. Robert Forster and Orest Ranum (Baltimore: John Hopkins University Press, 1982), pp. 95-127; see 117.

acts; Biblical texts were worn as amulets,[40] a phenomenon familiar to practitioners of traditional African religion.

But beyond their own innate sources of magic, Christian leaders showed a readiness to assimilate paganism into their own religious practice, rather than pose a conflict of loyalties to new converts.[41] The worship of wells, trees, and stones was transferred to the cults of Christian saints; the ancient festival of sun-worship at Midsummer Eve, complete with its pagan fire ceremony, became the Feast of St. John the Baptist. That this transferral never worked completely was evidenced by peculiar survivals: a bewitched cow could be cured by pouring holy water down its throat, while the fertility rites of May Day were only very imperfectly replaced by processions in honor of the Virgin Mary. Meanwhile, the church's own practices became more magical. As Keith Thomas observed, "the ceremonies of which [the church] disapproved were 'superstitious,' those which it accepted were not....It was the presence or absence of the Church's authority which determined the propriety of any action;"[42] and that authority was mediated through priests, many of whom were themselves a part of folk culture.

Until the seventeenth century, when a reform of seminary training was set in motion by the Council of Trent and by the new Protestant churches, parish clergy were more a part of the older, that is, of the folk religion than of the hierarchical one. Most parish priests were nearly as ignorant of doctrine and canon law as their parishioners. In 1520 a priest confessed to the Duke of Lorraine that "the majority of us [priests] are ignorant of the articles of faith." Even if the priesthood had been educated, however, the laity would not have profited, for, he continued, "in the Vosges mountains and in the mountains of Savoy there are so many simple folk who never hear their priest preach."[43] Given that fact, perhaps no more than forty percent of the population could be called Christian, judged by even the most minimal standard, that of receiving communion once a year at Easter. It was not that people were not religious: they practiced an emotional, even dramatic spirituality, keyed to their own crises and to the seasonal calendar of folk practice. But they largely ignored the Christian sacraments and calendar. What Toussaert

40. Geoffrey Parrinder, *Religion in Africa* (Baltimore: Penguin Books, 1969), p. 64.

41. Keith Thomas, *Religion and the Decline of Magic*, p. 47. My following section draws on Thomas's chap. 2, "The Magic of the Medieval Church," and on Jacques Toussaert, *Le sentiment religieux en Flandre à le fin du moyen âge* (Paris, 1963).

42. Thomas, *Religion and the Decline of Magic*, p. 49.

43. The priest quoted in question, Jean Glapion, was quoted in *Revue du Nord* 47, no. 182 (July-September 1964):365; noted in Muchembled, "Witchcraft," p. 215.

concludes for late medieval Flanders–that it was Christian only in an official sense–holds true for Lorraine as well.[44]

The medieval church encouraged the people's dependency on magic by claiming that the very uttering of the words of the mass were efficacious, whether or not understood by people or priest, and that the mere repetition of holy words could bring about desired results. Already set aside by their role as exorcists and as sacred celibates, priests added to their magical aura the notion that their ritual pronunication of words could change bread into the body of Christ and grant sinners a shorter term in purgatory. Proliferating beliefs about consecrated objects, sacred words, special gestures, created "a plethora of sub-superstitions" around the sacraments that rendered the medieval church "a vast reservoir of magical power."[45] We may get a notion of the spiritual climate of that time by noticing its similarity to the way some Africans, upon first encountering Christianity, insisted that merely looking at the Bible, or touching it, brings the blessings and protection promised in the Gospel.[46]

In the middle ages, emphasis on the physical efficacy of the sacraments reached its height in the cult surrounding the Eucharist, as the laity's desire for concrete, personal forms of charisma forced a change in the church's sacramental theology. Beginning in the ninth century, the church maintained that a priest's magic power could change the symbol of Christ's body and blood into its actuality, a power absolutely unthinkable for a layman and therefore guaranteed to raise the priesthood's standing. This cult had attained its apogee in the orthodox, thirteenth-century movements of the Sacred Heart and the late medieval processions on Corpus Christi Day. It was based not on the church's original eucharistic concept of a love feast providing communion with Christ but on a quite different principle, that the human body could not only contain a creative spirit, a *daemon*, but could itself be a magical vessel, a *numen*. This belief was an article of faith taken from popular religion.

Women's bodies were believed to contain this power more than men's. The *virginal* female body, that is, had an enormous magical potential. As Marina Warner has aptly observed,

---

44. Jacques Toussaert, *Le sentiment religieux*....

45. Thomas, *Religion and the Decline of Magic*, p. 45. On the special qualities claimed for sacerdotal celibates, see Anne L. Barstow, *The Church before and after Celibacy* (New York: Crossroad Publishing Co., forthcoming).

46. Geoffrey Parrinder, *West African Religion*, 2nd ed. (New York: Barnes and Noble, 1961).

> [The female virgin] was magic because of the long Christian tradition that had held since the second century that the inviolate body of a woman was one of the holiest things possible in creation, holier than the chastity of a man, who anatomically cannot achieve the same physical image of spiritual integrity as a woman.[47]

The church made good use of this tradition in its cult of Mary; and Joan of Arc, as we shall see, capitalized fully on it in building up her image as an *inspirée*.

The body of a sexually active woman was another matter; at best tolerated in Christian theology, it was readily seen as a source of pollution, danger, and even evil. The ritual of the churching, or purification, of women, was a case in point. Although theologians emphasized the celebratory side of the rite, as a thanksgiving for a safe childbirth, the people held to its original Old Testament meaning of the cleansing of the impure female body. In some areas people and priests alike agreed that neither menstruating women nor those who had had intercourse the night before should be admitted to communion.[48] Joining belief in the potential evil of the female body to the fact that the majority of magic practitioners were women, the church eventually created the image of the witch as the female partner of Satan.

***

The church historian Français Le Brun has raised the question "whether the French countryside was ever really Christian" prior to the seventeenth century.[49] Certainly in Joan's day the old religion of magic, fetish, and cunning woman was still very much alive. Against competition and even persecution it held on. Whether because of some mysterious peasant conservatism (which I doubt) or because the religion of official Christianity, even after its own syncretic efforts, never met the needs of the people (more likely, I believe), the old religion maintained itself as an active, potent way of dealing with life and death. Despite all the intermixing, the spiritual milieu of Europe

---

47. Marina Warner, *Joan of Arc*, p. 24.

48. Thomas, *Religion and the Decline of Magic*, pp. 38-39, n. While Thomas drew his material from a tract of 1643, he observes that there were many medieval precedents for these attitudes.

49. Le Brun, in *La nouvelle histoire de l'église* (Paris: Seuill, 1968), 3:246, in a discussion of the religion of the laity before the Reformation which runs through pp. 232-254; quoted in Muchembled, "Witchcraft," p. 215.

remained that of "two religions."

What the church could not absorb it attempted to destroy. These efforts did not diminish in the late medieval centuries, but rather grew. In Lorraine as elsewhere the church strove to monitor reports of new miracles, to control the work of self-ordained prophets, and to condemn all cunning persons.[50] But the church's attempt to draw the line between good and bad (Christian and folk) magic, between white and black witches, failed. Because the two religious systems overlapped, these Christian distinctions were compromised, incomprehensible in people's minds.

There was persecution. The church's heightened hostility to deviant belief, as evidenced in its attacks on its own members who chose to worship God as they saw right, and on Jews and Muslims, had occupied much of the church's energy in the thirteenth and fourteenth centuries. The fifteenth century found the church running low on heretics and other scapegoats, and increasingly it looked within its own communities for the enemy, neighbor accusing neighbor of maleficium and of traffic with the devil. This transition from heresy-hunting to witch-hunting is important for our story, because Joan of Arc was caught in both. It is necessary to see how a struggle over magic underlay both forms of persecution. By 1400 the church was moving to a showdown with local wise women, home-grown prophets and visionaries who claimed their own direct channel to God. The issue was quite simply *who* could declare *what* spiritual experience to be authentic.

In describing how, from the early sixth century until the medieval period, prophets and miracle-workers arose spontaneously, independent of the church and often in competition with it, Peter Brown documents the roots of the latter persecutions, claiming that "nothing less than a conflict of views on the relation between man and nature" was at stake.[51] Although Brown misjudges the pagan milieu, which was far from the grey area he describes, he is right nonetheless that the balance of power lay with the institution, and that there were left in rural areas "men and women who had been pushed tragically to one side by the rise of the Christian church."[52] The problem of the *inspirée* was there from the beginning: the church set up human administrative structures in which power centered on the bishop, while visionary individuals, shut out from

50. E. Delcambre, *Le concept de la sorcellerie dans le Duché de Lorraine*, 3 vols. (Nancy, 1948-1951). See esp. vol. 3, chap. 16.

51. Peter Brown, *The Cult of the Saints*, p. 125.

52. Ibid., p. 124.

those structures, struggled to express their messages from God and to enact their missions elsewhere. Unless they received approbation and protection from priests, they were vulnerable to persecution. The arena in which they could act became smaller as the centuries passed; by 1400 it was becoming dangerous for a layman or laywoman to say, "God has spoken to me."

This multifaceted process worked itself out very slowly, folk religion at times exerting strong input into official Christianity, the organization at times turning on and persecuting local deviance. In a period of particular religious tension, such as the early fifteenth century, a lay person might well read the signs wrong. She might assume there would be a place in the official clerical mind for her prophecies when in fact there would be no tolerance at all.

What needs to be kept in mind in considering the events of Joan of Arc's life is that the points of contact between the two religions were frequently painful. And in the last centuries of the middle ages, as medieval civilization declined and began to disintegrate, these contacts grew increasingly disruptive and destructive. Joan began as a local visionary and mystic, flourished as a national hero and magic worker, and ended as a condemned heretic and witch. Analyzing her particular combination of mystical gifts and heretical tendencies will not only explain much about Joan that is usually consigned to her "uniqueness;" it will also throw light on the deep divisions in her society over what was acceptable spiritual practice, especially over what was allowed to the spiritually gifted woman. It is this ability to illumine the weak points, the sore places in the social fabric, that recommends the study of heretical mysticism to the historian.

A number of female prophets had been active in France in the decades preceding Joan's entry into public life. And stretching out behind them was a line of spiritually gifted women known as mystics, some of whom became heroines of a sort, others of whom were labelled heretical. Joan had a fully documented role ready made. Given her devotion to France and to the Dauphin, her spiritual tendencies carried her into the center of a political maelstrom. More than any other mediumistic woman, Joan's destiny led her center-stage. Much light can be shed on her "active mysticism" by considering the women whose lives had created the role which she most famously filled.

Chapter Two
Female Prophets: Joan as Mystic

A spirit and a vision are not, as the modern philosophy supposes, a cloudy vapour, or a nothing. They are organized and minutely articulated beyond all that the mortal and perishing nature can produce.
William Blake, c. 1809

Joan of Arc may not at first seem to fit our conventional understanding of mysticism. While it is true that by her own account her voices came to her suddenly, when and where *they* chose, and while they vouchsafed to her a special knowledge of a unique mission about which she could not have learned any other way, thus fulfilling two important criteria for mystical experience, still the peasant girl who led an army may not seem to twentieth-century eyes a proper mystic.

The problem lies, I suggest, not in Joan but in our limited ideas about mystics. Historical evidence indicates more numerous categories of mystical expression than are today commonly supposed. The more familiar modes, which focus on love and union (exemplified by Hadewijch of Antwerp, for instance, or Thérèse of Lisieux) and on contemplative knowledge and understanding (Ruysbroeck, for example, and Nicholas of Cusa),[1] should be seen alongside a pragmatic mysticism, sometimes called a mysticism of action, which receives through visionary channels instruction about how to respond to actual problems in the life of society.[2] It is this third mode which best fits Joan, the girl who, in response to revelation, went out into the world, seizing with both hands her opportunity to change the course of her country's history.

Asked which voice came first to her when she was about thirteen, Joan answered:

1. F.C. Happold, *Mysticism: A Study and an Anthology* (New York: Penguin Books, 1970), pp. 40-42.
2. Cf. Dag Hammarskjöld, *Markings* (New York: Knopf, 1964), p. 122: "The 'mystical experience.' Always *here* and *now*–in that freedom...in the midst of action. In our era the road to holiness necessarily passes through the world of action."

It was St. Michael: I saw him before my eyes; and he was not alone, but quite surrounded by the Angels of Heaven.

Asked if she saw St. Michael and these angels corporeally and in reality, she answered:

I saw them with my bodily eyes as well as I see you; and when they left me, I wept; and I fain would have had them take me with them too.

Asked whether, when she saw the voice coming to her, there was a light, she answered:

There was a great deal of light on all sides, as was most fitting.

And she added, to her examiner:

All the light does not come to you alone![3]

Joan is not to be separated from her voices. Like Blake four centuries later, Joan held her spirits to be more real than her companions, than her own body.[4]

The inspiration for the army of France, the "image of female heroism," as Warner called her, was a mystic who heard and saw emissaries from heaven. As Warner and most modern writing about her makes clear, we would prefer a heroine closer to modern standards of rationality,[5] but it is Joan of Arc and not some more recent or less religious woman who is our subject. Indeed, if we take an historical point of view, Joan's hearing and seeing divine messengers enables us to interpret her as belonging to a definite tradition of late

3. The trial, 27 February 1431; from Murray, pp. 25, 27.

4. Michael Davis, *William Blake: A New Kind of Man* (Berkeley: University of California Press, 1977).

5. Warner, for example, (*Joan of Arc: The Image of Female Heroism*) sees mystics as not concerned with the problems of this world, as useless in effecting the course of events; claiming furthermore that they are given to hysteria and morbid introspection, she separates Joan of Arc from the category of mystics: "Joan was not a mystic; her visions are always of tasks to be accomplished in the world...," p. 89; her attack on mysticism runs from pp. 78-89. By ignoring the contribution to medieval society of visionaries such as Hildegard of Bingen, Mary of Oignies (founder of the beguine movement), and the two Gertrudes and two Mechtilds of Helfta, Warner overlooks the considerable impact of women as "active mystics." See also Victoria Sackville-West, in the "Aftermath" to her biography of Joan: "Jeanne was neither an ecstatic nor a mystic, nor in any sense of the word a 'hysterical' person."

medieval mysticism. Far from being "unique," Joan stands in a line of female visionary prophets who arose in Europe in the late middle ages. In this chapter and the next, I propose to look at that tradition, especially as it pertained to lay women, and particularly in France. First, however, I shall offer some general observations about mysticism and use these to elucidate the kind of mystic Joan was.

In this investigation, I shall take at face value the testimony which Joan and other mystics gave about their visionary experiences. Our concern here is not with psychological interpretation; it is not even with religious questions, certainly not theological ones, except as these entered into the story of Joan in her time. Instead of psychological or theological analysis, I offer an historical one, to show what Joan experienced, how she and her contemporaries interpreted those experienes, how the experiences look when viewed in the context of fifteenth-century life and history, and what result came of them. I shall be particularly attentive to the implications of Joan's fate for women who, like her, could claim no other authority than that of intense religious experience.

✳✳✳

Mystical experience should be seen as a social phenomenon. Although such an experience may be in many ways unique, the ability to have it is learned from others, and it serves needs that are shared by one's community. The mystic speaks a language she has learned from the reported experience of others, a language understood by her contemporaries. She belongs to a recognized type, and she stands within a known tradition of visions and revelations.

This being so, mystical experience is characterized by a sharp contradiction, for although it is shaped and perhaps even generated by societal factors, it nevertheless results in an intensely individualized state of mind, so particular to the individual and the occasion that it is often felt to be incommunicable. A mystical experience is usually felt to have been involuntary, spontaneous, transient, derived not from social training but from "beyond;" and it is understood to have imparted a gift of new knowledge, some insight which could not have been gained any other way. As F.C. Happold points out, the mystic feels that he or she "has received a pure, direct vision of truth," without willing it to happen and without the assistance of intermediaries.[6]

---

6. Happold, pp. 35-39, 45-57. Happold errs in questioning ecstasy as an authentic component of mystical expression; it is an authentic but not essential part of the

Pre-occupied with the individual soul in communion with God, many discussions of Christian mysticism emphasize its ascetic other-worldliness. I must therefore make it plain that this quality, which has perhaps become the distinguishing feature of mysticism in the minds of modern readers, does not belong to the late medieval female mysticism that is relevant to Joan of Arc. Mysticism is not necessarily contemplative, anti-Sacramental, ecstatic, nor other-worldly. It does not inevitably lead to withdrawal, to a special knowledge of God or even a special experience of God. It may (or may not) include seeing visions, hearing voices, receiving the gifts of prophecy, of healing, and of paranormal physical abilities such as bearing stigmata, levitating, or returning from near-death.

Far from being other-worldly, mystical experience often has direct relevance to the social order. It is therefore frequently a subversive force. The mystic may not start out to challenge the power of the church, for example, but if the church attacks one for one's vision of truth, one must defend the authenticity of that revelation. Mysticism is inherently anti-authoritarian. Always endowing the subject with certainty that her vision is true, it may force her into a social or political conflict she had not sought.

Joan exemplifies an aspect of mystical experience that is highly relevant to historical research about autonomous women: the receiving of insight not available through ordinary social channels. She represents the kind of mystic who receives instructions about the unraveling of a problem, sometimes the re-patterning of knowledge, together with a sense of absolute authority about both the source and the rightness of this knowledge. Through such a channel an otherwise disempowered woman might receive instructions previously unheard of by those of her age, gender, or class. She might, for example, receive a message of radical, non-conformist criticism of church or society. She might be given original views quite independent of accepted opinion. Joan's message was unacceptable, ultimately, to the most powerful forces in her society, and she was confronted then with the final command that authoritarian power can make: sacrifice *your* vision for *our* version of the truth.

***

In Joan's case, one must first observe that her accounts of her visions come entirely from her trial. Rendered under threat of death, they are often inconclusive and sometimes contradictory.

mystical experience. See I.M. Lewis, *Ecstatic Religion*, chap. 1.

While fending with some of the sharpest theological minds in France, all in the pay of the English and hostile to her from the start, she was of course not able to provide us with neat definitions of her types of religious experience. Much about them, therefore, must remain unanswered. Given that she had already been imprisoned for nine months when the trial began, was shackled in iron chains, and was weakened by a Lenten fast, Joan's sustained audacity, sharpness of mind, and even humor are remarkable.

About mystical experience one should ask ordinary questions: where, when, how often, accompanied by what, and in what forms did the manifestations occur? Joan's description of the first appearance of her "counsel" indicates that it took her by surprise and was not entirely welcome:

> I was thirteen when I had a Voice from God for my help and guidance. The first time that I heard the voice I was very much frightened; it was mid-day, in the summer, in my father's garden.

The Augustinian ring of these words places Joan's visitation in the classic tradition of Christian mystical experience, as does her next comment:

> ...rarely do I hear it without its being accompanied also by a light....Generally it is a great light.[7]

Similar, although not identical, luminous experiences are claimed by Eskimo shamans, by the Hindu Arjuna, by visionary Spanish peasants, by the beguine mystics Hadewijch of Antwerp and Marguerite Porete, by the orthodox mystic Theresa of Avila.[8] "The ravishing

---

7. Murray, p. 10. The tender age at which Joan's visions began is not unusual. William Christian reminds us that in our time children as young as eight or so have had visions at Fatima and Lourdes, and one of the medieval visionaries whom he describes was twelve-and-a-half: see William A. Christian, Jr. *Apparitions in Late Medieval and Renaissance Spain* (Princeton: Princeton University Press, 1981), pp. 36, 57. Other examples of precocious spiritual awakening are: Margaret of Ypres, five; Hadewijch of Antwerp, ten; Catherine of Siena, ten; Mechtild of Magdeburg, twelve; Christine of Stommeln, "as far back as my memory can reach." See Ernest McDonnell, *Beguines and Beghards in Medieval Culture*, (1954; New York: Octagon Books, 1969), pp. 86-88.

8. Marguerite Porete, *A Mirror for Simple Souls*, by an anonymous thirteenth-century French mystic (sic) trans. C. Crawford (New York: Crossroad Publishing Co., 1981), pp. 133-135; Hadewijch, *The Complete Works*, trans. Mr. Columba Hart (New York: Paulist Press, 1980), pp. 90, 118; Theresa of Avila, *The Life*, trans. J. Cohen (London, 1957), pp. 197-198; Eliade, *Shamanism*, pp. 60-61, 420.

flash of divine light" bringing inner illumination, appears frequently to monastic mystics, but it is typical of Joan's forthright nature that she experienced the light as most lay visionaries do, outwardly and concretely, "coming in the name of the voice" or "the same time as the voice" or even "in front of the voice."[9] In all of her testimony, Joan represented her voices as phenomena not only heard with her ears but seen with her eyes.

She claimed that she saw them every day, sometimes three times a day, sometimes more. They appeared to her in the woods, in church, in battle, in the courtroom, in her cell where her guards made so much noise that she could not properly follow what the voices were saying to her.[10] She often heard them when bells were ringing, "chiefly at Compline or Matins," and when they did not ring, she missed them; she asked the church warden at Domremy to ring the bells more often, and when she had joined the army she requested the chaplains to ring the bells for half an hour on end. Her neighbors reported that often when she was in the fields and heard the bells, she would drop to her knees.[11] They assumed she was saying her prayers, but Joan was in fact listening for her voices; she had become dependent on them.

Sometimes she referred to the voices in the singular, as her "counsel," and she apparently never identified it as two saints and an archangel until she was examined by Charles' theologians at Poitiers. Because that record is lost, we must depend on her guarded answers at the Rouen examination for descriptions of her apparitions.

Although St. Catherine came to Joan most often and appeared to be closest to her, it was, she finally admitted, the archangel and saint Michael who appeared to her in the first visitation. Venerated in Lorraine at a pilgrimage spot not far from Domremy,[12] it was Michael who told Joan "of the great misery there was in the kingdom of France" and who first instructed her to go there.[13]

This is Michael the mighty standard bearer who will lead the dead into the holy light, who can rescue souls from Hell, who is portrayed in medieval art as weighing souls in order to judge them. It is Michael the warrior, slaying the dragon, whose great shrine at Mont St. Michel never surrendered to the English. It was he whom Joan invoked at the stake, the first and the last of her apparitions. When

---

9. Barrett, p. 62; Murrary, p. 18; Tisset-Lanhers, 1:62, gives the French as "au devant de la voix."

10. Murray, pp. 62, 64, 16, 22, 306.

11. Ibid., pp. 149-150, 215, 218, 220, 221, 240.

12. Marot, *Joan the Good Lorrainer*, p. 44.

13. Murray, p. 85.

she beseeched his aid as her body was being burned, she may well have recalled the claim that it was Michael who had cooled the furnace blast for Daniel.[14]

Catherine and Margaret, the two female saints, apparently always appeared together, although Joan refused to be specific about this. St. Margaret of Antioch was, like Michael, often depicted stabbing a dragon, but in a story more reminiscent of Joan's own broken betrothal than Michael's fierce encounter. The most popular medieval compilation of miraculous tales, *The Golden Legend*, recounts the story as follows: imprisoned at the age of fifteen, Margaret made a dragon vanish by the sign of the cross. The dragon returned and swallowed her, but she escaped by making it burst (a reference to childbirth?). When the dragon reappeared as a young man courting her, she threw him to the ground, placed her foot on his body and boasted, "'Proud demon, lay prostrate beneath a woman's foot.' And he could but moan, 'O Margaret, I am conquered! And to complete my humiliation, my conqueror is a young girl, whose parents were my friends.'"[15] Margaret was no gentle saint.

Margaret was also valued as guardian of those in childbirth: the woman who invoked her would come through her ordeal safely and so would her child. Joan must certainly have felt close to this saint at the time of her law suit over her refusal to marry the young man who charged her with breach of promise, for Margaret too refused a forced marriage, for which she was tortured, tempted, and finally beheaded. Before her death, Margaret's preaching converted throngs to Christianity.[16] The statue of her which Joan knew in the church at Domremy is still there.

The saint who most often spoke to Joan, with whom she felt close enough to argue, was St. Catherine, "whom I love so much." The church in the neighboring village of Maxey-sur-Meuse was dedicated to Catherine and contained an image of her. Catherine too was a virgin who refused marriage because of her vow to Christ, for which she was tortured on a wheel and martyred. Even more to the point for Joan, who would face an inquisitional court, Catherine had debated against fifty pagan philosophers and triumphed over them, becoming thereby the patron of students, the clergy, and philosophers.[17]

14. *Oxford Dictionary of Saints*, ed. D.H. Farmer (Oxford: Oxford University Press, 1978), pp. 277-278; *New Catholic Encyclopedia*, pp. 793-794; Jacopus de Voraigne, *The Golden Legend*, trans. G. Ryan and H. Rippenberger (New York: Longmans, Green, & Co., 1941), 2:578-586.

15. Jacopus de Voraigne, *The Golden Legend*, 2:351-354.

16. *ODS*, pp. 69-70; *NCE*, pp. 199-200.

As we shall see (Chapter Three), it was Catherine's shrine at Fierbois that miraculously furnished Joan with the sword she carried through all her victories, and legends about the shrine's furnishing magical escape for condemned prisoners may have inspired Joan's belief that her voices would save her from the death sentence at Rouen. Echoes of many details about Catherine found in *The Golden Legend* may have influenced Joan's visions: that when Catherine debated the pagans, an angel stood by her; that when her pagan converts were burned at the stake, "not a hair of their heads nor a shred of their garments suffered the least harm;" that when she was imprisoned in a cell without food, Christ fed her by an angel; and that one of her symbols was a crown. One of Catherine's fingers was reputed to be in the reliquary at Rouen.[18]

One gets the picture of a lively Christianity informing the mind of the young Joan through legends well-known across Europe. This is folk Christianity, not the same as the faith of councils, bishops, and popes. Both of Joan's female saints were later dismissed from the Roman calendar, and neither had been heard of in the West before the ninth century. Catherine and Margaret are examples of Patrick Geary's thesis that during Carolingian times the Roman church was forced to produce new saints. In order to accommodate the people's reliance on magic-working heroes and heroines, the church canonized legendary Eastern figures, giving them some of the characteristics of local miracle workers, Celtic, for example, Germanic or Tuscan.[19] Catherine and Margaret as Joan knew them no doubt exhibited aspects of popular ancient miracle-workers, more powerful than loving, practical and hard-headed rather than sweet.

Joan was unusual in not having visions of the Virgin Mary, who was by all odds the most popular spectral visitor in medieval, as in modern, times. That she was visited instead by Michael, Catherine and Margaret attest to the potency of their legends in Lorraine, to their particular usefulness to a young patriot in time of national distress, and their appropriateness for an independent-minded woman. But in any event, Joan exhibited no especial affinity for the usual icons of Mary, those representations of her as mother of Christ.

Joan was not at all atypical, however, in the manner of her belief in her voices. By taking them literally, by setting her life-course by their admonitions, she followed a vigorous tradition. As R.W.

17. *ODS*, pp. 69-70; *NCE*, p. 253.
18. *The Golden Legend*, 1:708-716; Murray, p. 29.
19. Geary, "The Ninth-Century Relic Trade," as discussed above in chap. 1.

Southern observed of medieval popular religion, "The deficiencies in human resouces were supplied by the power of the saints; they were great power houses in the fight against evil."[20] If an illiterate peasant girl was intent on becoming the savior of her country, what better resource could she have?

The messages given by Joan's guides were very specific. Following upon Michael's initial admonition that she must go to France, they told her to wear men's clothes, that her sword would be found at Fierbois, that she would be wounded at Orléans, that Catherine de La Rochelle was a fraud, that Joan would be captured, would suffer, but would escape.[21] They promised her that de Baudricourt would give her an escort, that the king would recognize her at Chinon, that she would raise the siege of Orléans, and that the king would regain his kingdom.[22] Ever since Joan had proven herself at Orléans, the voices had called her the Daughter of God. Having forbidden her to try to escape from Beaurevoir, they nonetheless comforted her when she leaped from the tower and injured herself. They threatened that if she revealed their secrets to anyone without their permission, they would leave her. And they assured her that she would go to Paradise.[23]

For her part, Joan was specific about the authoritative source of these audacious prophecies. She declared on the third day of her trial that "the Voice comes to me from God." Joan held to this belief through fierce interrogation. Although when faced with immolation she denied this affirmation once, she immediately took back her recantation, reasserting that her Voices came from God, and that what she had done had been by God's command. When asked if she believed she was in a state of mortal sin, she affirmed that she could not be, for how else would her voices continue to come to her?[24]

* * *

Joan's judges took close interest in whether she maintained active, conscious control during her mystical encounters. On the matter of whether she summoned her voices or they her, Joan's statements are ambiguous in the extreme. When asked about it, her reply,

20. R.W. Southern, *The Making of the Middle Ages* (London: Penguin Books, 1973), p. 137.

21. Murray, pp. 12, 32, 41, 53, 57, 75-76.

22. Ibid., pp. 23, 41, 77.

23. Ibid., p. 76.

24. Ibid., pp. 17, 356; 18, 370.

> They often come without being called; and other times, if they do not come soon, I pray our Lord to send them....I have never had need of them without having them,[25]

leads us to assume that Joan was in control, able to summon her spirits when needed. And yet we learn that they often appeared to her spontaneously, awakening her from sleep, for example, and surprising and frightening her in their first visitation. The contradiction is only apparent, for to medieval villagers, "both communities and saints were reaching out to communicate with each other."[26] The saints took some initiatives themselves, sending portents and working miracles, but the surest way of getting through was by identifying themselves and delivering messages through apparitions. Persons such as Joan, gifted at reading these signs, served their communities as the mediums for messages in times of impending danger.

As to the question whether Joan maintained control of her will while in contact with her voices, Joan's reports indicate again that she remained an active agent in the encounter, arguing with them and even disobeying them.

For instance, when the voices took too long to bring about the help that Joan needed, she took matters into her own hands. Imprisoned at Beaurevoir after her capture at Compiègne, Joan almost killed herself by jumping from the tower in an attempt at escape. Before taking this desperate step, however, Joan got into the following argument with St. Catherine:

> Saint Catherine told me almost every day not to leap, that God would help me, and also those [besieged] at Compiègne. I said to Saint Catherine: 'Since God will help those at Compiègne, I wish to be there.' Saint Catherine said to me, 'Be resigned, and do not falter: you will not be delivered before seeing the King of England.' I answered her: 'Truly I do not wish to see him; I would rather die than fall into the hands of the English.'[27]

Joan had argued with her voices before. Protesting to St. Michael, for instance, that she could not take up the call to go to France because she knew nothing of fighting, she had put off obeying. But her voices hounded her; for five years they pursued her, and finally

25. Murray, p. 62.
26. Christian, *Apparitions...in Spain*, p. 15.
27. Murray, p. 74.

she had complied. When her judges ridiculed her for letting herself be captured outside the walls at Compiègne, implying that her voices, if from God, should have saved her, Joan half-admitted that they could have done more. Confessing that the voices had indeed prophesied that she would be captured but had not told her the day or hour, she admitted that:

> If I had known the hour when I should be taken, I should never have gone [outside Compiègne] of my own free-will; I should always have obeyed their commands....[28]

Joan stressed her obedience to her voices, but we see that when left with insufficient guidance Joan acted of her own free-will, in this case rashly and with tragic consequences. Joan admitted that she sometimes took the initiative. Refusing for the third of many times to tell her judges what was the magical sign she showed to the King, she allowed that she had promised her saints "without their asking it of me, of my own free-will" not to divulge that sign to anyone. And only under the most insistent questioning near the end of her trial did she do so.

As to whether Joan retained conscious control of herself or lost herself in trance, Andrew Lang was convinced that she retained her consciousness and common sense while hearing the voices. Unlike subjects in trance, she did not dissociate or hallucinate, remaining instead fully alert, even vigilant. Far from becoming the voices' passive instrument, she was their loyal but often skeptical co-worker. As William Christian, Jr., has shown, lay mystics, in contrast to nuns and *beatas* or beguines, were almost never ecstatics. They did not experience trance, and perhaps because they were visited by their apparitions in private, they had no need of extravagant signs of behavior.[29]

Although in these matters Joan was typical of other lay adepts, she did experience ecstatic moments with her voices. Count de Dunois recalled years later that after the success at Orléans, the king and two clerics had asked her to describe her "counsel." Blushing, Joan had replied that:

28. Ibid., p. 58.

29. Andrew Lang, *The Maid of France, Being the Story of the Life and Death of Jeanne d'Arc* (New York: Longman's Green and Co., 1909), pp. 46-47. Christian, *Apparitions...in Spain*, pp. 186-187.

When I am vexed that faith is not readily placed in what I wish to say in God's Name, I retire alone, and pray to God. I complain to Him that those whom I address do not believe me more readily; and, my prayer ended, I hear a Voice which says to me: 'Daughter of God! go on! go on! go on! I will be thy Help: go on!' And when I hear this Voice, I have great joy. I would I could always hear it thus.

Dunois finished by commenting that "in repeating to us the language of her Voice, she was–strange to say!–in a marvellous rapture, raising her eyes to Heaven."[30] And a priest at Vaucouleurs remembered that when he had seen her "a long time in prayer," on her knees in the crypt of the castle chapel, "sometimes her face [was] bent to the ground, **sometimes** raised to heaven."[31] While Joan's consciousness did not dissolve into trance, still she knew about spiritual rapture.

Perhaps the perplexing issue of mystical passivity versus activity, of supernatural versus human initiative, can be resolved by turning to Meister Eckhart's description of the human/divine encounter. In a sermon on why God became a human being, the fourteenth-century German mystic considered that the human spirit "has to go beyond all quantity and break through all diversity. Then it will be broken through by God." Then, sounding very much like Joan arguing with her saints, Eckhart continued, "Quite the same way, however, as God breaks through me, I shall break through him in return!" Continually elaborating on the interaction between God and humanity, he allowed humans an autonomous role, or at least an autonomous moment.

Yet Eckhart's training as a Dominican **theologian** brings him back to the mainstream of Catholic thought when he claims that "God does not *force* the will. He rather places it in freedom in such a way that it wishes nothing other than what God wishes. This is not its lack of freedom; it is its innate freedom."[32] The deep ambiguities embedded in this classic statement of Christian freedom close out the possibility for autonomous human action. I would suggest that Joan's experiences represented the mystical, active (and heretical) side of Eckhart's thought rather than its more orthodox strain.

30. Murray, pp. 238-239.

31. Ibid., p. 231.

32. Meister Eckhart, Sermon 25, "Our Divinity: The Reason God Became a Human Being," in *Breakthrough: Meister Eckhart's Creation Spirituality in New Translation,* ed. Matthew Fox, O.P. (Garden City: Doubleday and Co., 1980), p. 355.

***

Except for one brief period of recantation when sentenced to death, Joan was steadfast in witness to her voices as real and as messengers of God. In having such experiences and such convictions, she was not alone. There was, for example, Pieronne of Brittany, whose story parallels Joan's in important ways; her unwavering faith in her visions brought her condemnation by the Parisian inquisition one year before Joan. Pieronne's path crossed that of Joan at Jargeau on the Loire, where both women took communion from Brother Richard on Christmas Day, 1429. Along with the visionary Catherine de La Rochelle, whom we shall meet again, they were considered to be followers of the wandering preacher.[33] Pieronne was captured by the English at Corbeil with another woman[34] and held for six months in Paris.

The Bourgeois reported that Pieronne maintained that "God often appeared to her in human form and talked to her as one friend does to another; that the last time she had seen him he was wearing a long white robe with a red tunic underneath," that whenever the precious body of Our Lord was consecrated "she would see the great secret wonders of Our Lord God."[35] This vision was declared blasphemous, and, refusing to recant of her claim that she frequently saw God in this way, Pieronne was condemned and burned at the stake. That Pieronne had proclaimed Joan (now in prison) good and her actions the will of God, cannot have helped Joan's case.

While it is difficult to separate theological from political motives in Pieronne's trial, the theological point was made that talking with God as a friend was heresy. What the church would not tolerate, in Pieronne's case as in Joan's, was the individual's claim to special communication with the divine. In its endeavor to control spiritual life, the church had to guard against individual revelations.

A well-known nun of ⌜Joan's time, St. Colette, also received visions, but of an ecclesiastical nature. While living as a lay recluse and practising severe austerities, she received divine instruction to reform the order of Poor Clares (the female branch of the

33. Bourgeois, pp. 253-254.
34. Vauchez, in "Les Soeurs de Jeanne," is wrong to assume that Pieronne *fought* for the Armagnacs; the text of the Bourgeois does not warrant that translation. She must have been instead a follower of theirs, possibly through her devotion to Br. Richard, or her admiration for Joan, or simply from her hatred of the English, who were trying to annex her homeland, Brittany.
35. Bourgeois, p. 265.

Franciscans). Going a bit further than her visions may have intended, she established twenty new convents and an entire new order, the Coletans. Famed for her extreme asceticism, she soon attracted royal attention: she was consulted for over forty years by the mother of the duke of Burgundy and was employed during the Schism as negotiator with her patron the antipope Felix V.[36] Because Joan stayed for a short while in Colette's convent at Moulin, it is likely that they met, but we have no record of what passed between them. Like Joan, Colette enjoyed aristocratic favor and considerable local fame; unlike Joan, Colette received the cooperation and respect of the church, providing the wisdom of submitting one's visions to the authorities and of joining an order.

An impressive group of female mystics, while not taking a direct role, as Joan did, in the political life of their times, were nonetheless active mystics, serving as channels for criticism of the church. Perhaps "criticism" is not the precise word, for several of them, like Joan, did not intend to attack the church. Yet because they made known their visions, all were attacked by the church, and in defending the truth of their visions, all were forced to become its critics. In the process, all ran afoul of the inquisition, that tribunal of the church founded in the early thirteenth century to stamp out heresy.[37]

One of the first women to be condemned by the inquisition for her visions, the French-speaking prophet Marguerite Porete, was burned at the stake in Paris in 1310. The religious milieu in which she functioned, that of the lay convents known as beguinages, reveals much about the motivation of female lay mystics; its history informs us of the heritage of independent lay spirituality available to Joan, whereas its fate explains the paucity of the religious options left to women in her time.

36. *Vita Sanctae Coletae 1381-1447*, ed. Yves Cozaux, et al. (Leiden: Brill, 1982), pp. 141-143.

37. In *The Repression of Heresy in Medieval Germany* (Philadelphia: University of Pennsylvania Press, 1979), Richard Kieckhefer offers convincing evidence for not viewing the papal inquisition as either monolithic or particularly effective before the seventeenth century, observing that the local episcopal inquisitional efforts achieved more. I would argue only that the existence, beginning in 1233, of special papal legislation for heresy trials, decreeing extra harsh measures for such courts, had the same effect on all judicial action against alleged heretics, whether papal, episcopal, or even municipal. The court that Joan faced was co-presided over by a bishop and the papal vice-inquisitor for France, and followed the legal instructions for an inquisitional (that is, an antiheretical) court. It made small difference to the accused whether a bishop or a papal legate tried her under those instructions.

For about a century before Marguerite's time there had been a noticeable spiritual restlessness among the urban women in northern Europe. Either unable to enter convents because they lacked the necessary dowry, or unwilling to submit themselves to the increasingly rigid control and narrow life style of those institutions, large numbers of spiritually gifted women had begun to form lay communities of their own. A lay, middle-class response to the great religious revival of the High Middle Ages, beguinages began to appear around 1200 in the cities and towns of Flanders and spread across northern France and the Rhineland. These devout women owed no obedience to outside authority, neither to abbess, priest, nor bishop, an independence they sustained through their economic self-reliance; being entirely voluntary and non-institutional, their spirituality stressed inner, personal forms. Having thus established a spiritual base for themselves, beguines relied less on the guidance of priests than did other groups of religious women.[38]

Out of this movement emerged a distinctive female spirituality and, as Caroline Bynum has documented, a female subculture.[39] When women created a space in which they could function autonomously, they did not simply replicate male culture but built distinctive communities. Whether as beguinages or as Cistercian or Dominican convents, these female communities were less authoritarian, less structured by legal concepts and hierarchical roles than the male orders; conversely they placed more value on "the experiences of the heart," on what we call mystical gifts. They produced leaders whose authority came from their visions, whose spiritual life was more mystical than that of men in religious life, with strong emphasis on paranormal experiences–visions, voices, stigmata, miraculous cures, even levitation and return from near-death.[40]

38. Having been prevented from forming new religious orders by the Lateran decree of 1215, devout burgher women gathered in loosely organized hostels to lead lives of communal worship, daily manual labor, and chastity. Each unit was entirely self-contained; typically, they confessed to the woman they chose as their leader, and read the Scriptures in the vernacular and commented on them. Ernest McDonnell, *Beguines and Beghards in Medieval Culture*, (1954; New York: Octagon Books, 1969), pp. 366-367 and pt. 2, chap. 5; pt. 2, chaps. 7-8; and pt. 3, chap. 3, esp. p. 321.

39. Caroline W. Bynum, *Jesus as Mother: Studies in the Spirituality of the High Middle Ages* (Berkeley: University of California Press, 1982) chap. 5, "Women Mystics in the Thirteenth Century: The Case of the Nuns of Helfta;" and "Was There a Female Subculture Among Women Religious in the Later Middle Ages?", paper delivered at Barnard College, New York City, 1 November 1980. My thanks to Professor Bynum for sharing this research with me. Bynum observes that this spirituality, highly Christo-centric, focused on Christ's wounds, his humanity, his role as counsellor, friend, bridegroom, lover; receiving the Eucharist was, therefore, a central desire.

Bynum finds that these women's mystical visions rendered them "chains linking others to God, mediators in whose merits others may participate...[who] are convinced of the necessity of teaching others the truths revealed to them in visions...."[41] In short, they saw themselves as entirely worthy to be channels of divine messages, and as seers, fully capable of revealing to others the desires of their hearts. And many persons, including priests and the nobility, came to these gifted diviners for counsel. We can say that there was, from the early thirteenth century on, a role in European society for the spiritually graced woman, whether lay or religious.

The lay women, however, were not accepted by the papacy, and because they were not under ecclesiastical supervision, they were the first of all visionary groups to be attacked.[42] Papal censures[43] led up to Pope Clement V's decisive decrees of 1311, which proclaimed the dissolution of the beguine movement and listed eight heretical errors,[44] propositions probably taken (out of context) from Marguerite Porete's trial the year before. Several of these "errors" became propositions used to catch Joan out at her trial, namely, that a person can achieve perfection, that in this state she is incapable of sin, and that she can therefore dispense with the church's ministrations.

Once papal hostility was official, the beguines' local enemies were empowered. Several beguines were burned at the stake for heresy, and much of the beguinage property was confiscated. By the end of the fourteenth century the movement was virtually ended; the remaining beguine convents "had been reduced to poor houses whose inmates no longer busied themselves with theological questions,"[45] nor, presumably, with daring visions. Joan's type of mysticism led her in directions quite different from that found in these communities of women, but we should note that the one great insti-

40. Brenda M. Bolton, "Vitae Matrum: A Further Aspect of the Frauenfrage," in *Medieval Women*, ed. Derek Baker (Oxford: Oxford University Press, 1978), pp. 253-268.

41. Bynum, *Jesus as Mother*.

42. McDonnell, *Beguines and Beghards*, p. 341. As early as 1210 they were forbidden to preach, and by 1249 a local council ruled that they must not translate Scripture, comment on it, nor write books.

43. Herbert Grundmann, *Religiöse Bewegungen im Mittelalter*, 2nd ed. (Hildesheim, 1961), pp. 333-340. In the pope's presence in 1274 the beguines were attacked for refusing obedience to parish clergy and for publicly disseminating their religious insights.

44. Hefele-Leclercq, *Histoire des conciles* (Paris, 1907-1938), pt. 2, 6:681-684.

45. McDonnell, *Beguines and Beghards*, p. 573; on the deaths, pp. 490-492, 500, 561, 565; on confiscation, pp. 564-565.

tution of female lay piety which she might have entered had been almost entirely destroyed before her lifetime.

Because the independence of thought and action of many of these lay mystics was as extraordinary as Joan's, it is worthwhile to look at their lives. The first to come to the attention of the inquisitor of Paris, Marguerite Porete was a wandering preacher who, by the mid-1290s had written *A Mirror for Simple Souls*, a book describing what she had learned of the mystical ascent and the vision of God.[46] At some time before 1306 the book was condemned and burned in her presence at Valenciennes, and she was threatened with death if she spread her ideas further.

Marguerite describes a state of grace in which the soul, no longer needing good works, is no longer dependent on the church. Defining the church as something "made," man-made, that is, Marguerite ultimately rejected it, in order to make room for ecstatic union with God.[47]

The inquisitor who imprisoned Marguerite lifted her statements out of context, and sent a summary to a theological commission for judgment, thereby setting a precedent for the unfair procedure used against Joan a century later. The summary implied, for example, that Marguerite claimed that one could, without qualification, grant nature all that it asked.[48] The judgment against her was based also on her denial of need for the Eucharist, prayers, sermons, poverty, fasts, or any penance. While not denying that the virtues and the

---

46. Marguerite Porete, *A Mirror for Simple Souls.* The only modern English translation, and only edition in print, is wrongly ascribed to "an anonymous thirteenth-century mystic," and the author is referred to repeatedly as male. Trans. Charles Crawford (New York: Crossroad Publishers, 1981). For a description of how Marguerite's name was first dropped and, six hundred years later, reunited with her book, see Anne L. Barstow, review of *A Mirror for Simple Souls*, in *Religious Studies Review*, 1983, and Robert E. Lerner, *The Heresy of the Free Spirit in the Later Middle Ages* (Berkeley: University of California Press, 1972), pp. 1-2, 7-8, 71-79, 200-208.

47. As for why the Church does not recognize these royal souls, Marguerite concludes sadly that it "cannot recognize them without entering into their souls, and there is no room in their souls for anything made, but only for God, who made them." *A Mirror for Simple Souls*, p. 58.

48. Henry C. Lea, *A History of the Inquisition*, 2:122-123, with trial documents. Marguerite had in fact written that in a state of grace, the soul knows no intermediary between itself and God, is united with the Trinity, finds God wherever it looks, can even find God within itself. Since the liberated Soul is so well aligned with virtue, Marguerite can boldly claim to give to nature, without remorse, all that it asks— because nature will no longer ask anything that it should not. It is little wonder that a theological commission, having read a list of truncated formulations, found Marguerite to be heretical and that contemporaries soon associated her with the most extreme libertine statements alleged against some of the Free Spirit groups.

offices of what she called "Church the Little" could bring salvation, Marguerite had made it clear that the liberated Soul could only be hampered by such distractions, and had thereby invited the charge of self-sufficiency. The antinomian accusation, however, was a clear misreading of her text.

Although there is no biography of Marguerite, it appears that she did not live in a community, had no confessor or spiritual director, followed no charismatic preacher.[49] On the contrary, she was on the move, teaching in or sending her book to Valenciennes, Chalons, Tournai, Paris. If, having been warned, Marguerite had been willing to enter a convent, she might have saved herself, but she seems to have been fearless: ordered to show her book to no one, she promptly sent it to three theologians for their approval, which she got.[50] In both her independence and her unwavering belief in her mission, Marguerite was her own woman.

While Marguerite's visions were related to her union with God, another beguine in southern France was visited by God and by Jesus "in the form of a man and in his divinity," not so that she might be absorbed into God but in order that she might receive an astonishing message about the church.[51] Jesus came to Prous Boneta in church as the priest raised the eucharistic elements of Christ's body and blood, infusing her with a feeling of great warmth; afterwards when she was alone in the cemetery, Jesus surrounded her with radiant light and showed her his pierced heart, and she gave him her love. God told her that the world was in the grip of Antichrist, who was, in fact, the pope, John XXII. Prous' message maintained that since John had taken over the rule of Christendom, the sacraments had lost their efficacy and would never regain them as long as he

49. She shares with her contemporary Meister Eckhart a crucial belief in the nonexistence of sin as well as the image of the soul handing itself over to God without will, as an empty receptacle who is allowed nothing. Some scholars believe that Marguerite may well have influenced Eckhart. Wolfgang Riehle, *Studien zur englischen Mystik des Mittelalters* (Heidelberg, 1977), pp. 48, 229; Lerner, *The Heresy of the Free Spirit*, p. 183. A clear legacy from Marguerite, however, was the concept of the soul's dark night, or "far night," as she called it, later brought to its fullest expression by John of the Cross.

50. While Marguerite apparently did not involve herself in politics, she did write two opinions that could well have been taken as criticisms of King Philip the Fair's government (Lerner, *The Heresy of the Free Spirit*, p. 77). On the question of Marguerite's orthodoxy, see Eleanor McLaughlin, "The Heresy of the Free Spirit and Late Medieval Mysticism," *Medievalia et Humanistica*, n.s. 4 (1973):37-54.

51. William H. May, "The Confession of Prous Boneta, Heretic and Heresiarch," in *Essays in Medieval Life and Thought* (New York: Columbia University Press, 1955), pp. 3-30. The confession itself is on pp. 7-30.

was pope.

This attack on John XXII identifies Prous with the Spiritual Franciscans, and indeed, one of the radical friars was imprisoned by the inquisition with her. But there is no need to speculate about Prous' connections, for she revealed to the inquisitor her entire message: that God had prepared for the defeat of Antichrist through the life and teachings of Peter John Olivi, the Franciscan radicals' hero, and was now ready to redeem mankind again, this time through Prous—if only the world would heed her message. Just as God had ruled the world through the two fleshly bodies of Christ and his mother, so he will now rule it through the two spiritual bodies of Olivi and Prous. She completed this astonishing proclamation by claiming that God had chosen her to be the incarnation of the Holy Ghost! Just as Eve had caused the ruin of the human race, so Prous, like the Virgin Mary, would bring about its salvation.

Prous was condemned by the inquisition in 1325 at Carcasonne, turned over to the secular arm, and presumably burned at the stake. For Prous, Olivi's condemnation had been the turning point in history, and she was its new fulfillment.[52] This extreme prophetic claim, more dramatic then anything envisioned by a male mystic, is proof that women were capable of seeing themselves in dramatic roles, indeed, in the central role in the cosmic drama of salvation.[53]

The one other French woman who ran afoul of the inquisition in this period, Jeanne (or Péronne) Dabenton, apparently was not a visionary. Her error seems to have been her leadership of a devout group called "Turlupins," who espoused holy poverty and who probably offended by being lay itinerant preachers. She was burned in

52. Although few persons seem to have believed in Prous's messianic view of herself (the friar who had been arrested with her denied the truth of her visions and was released), many, including the Franciscan de Roquetaillade, were influenced, as was she, by Olivi's Joachite vision of a new age in history. See my chapter 3.

53. A dramatic example of extreme prophetic claims by a woman occurred in Milan c. 1271: one Guglielma appeared, gathering followers, including relatives of the powerful Visconti family, claiming that she was the incarnation of the Holy Spirit. She would rise from the dead, ascend bodily into heaven, and send back upon her disciples the Holy Spirit as tongues of flame. Having thus established herself as the new Christ figure, Guglielma condemned Boniface VIII as no true pope and declared that ecclesiastical authority was dead. In order to revive it, the pope and the cardinals must be women! The female pope (one of Guglielman's disciples, Manfreda) would baptize all infidels and claim the Holy See in a peaceable manner. On Guglielma, see Marjorie Reeves, *Joachim of Fiore and the Prophetic Future* (New York, 1977), p. 50, and n. 68. Reeves calls the sect "mad" and "absurd;" one can ask if the Gugliemites' claims were any more extreme than those of Boniface VIII. A more sympathetic interpretation can be found in Stephen E. Wessley, "The Thirteenth-Century Guglielmites: Salvation Through Women," in Derek Baker, ed. *Medieval Women*, pp. 289-303.

Paris in 1372, along with a male colleague who had died in prison two weeks earlier but whose body had been preserved in lime for this final rite of humiliation.[54]

The secular authorities were from that time on to show more appreciation for the political uses of the inquisitional tribunal,[55] while taking care to assert the power of the local courts over those of the papal inquisition.[56] Bishops, after all, were more local in their loyalties; inquisitors were appointed by, and were too responsive to, Rome.

In Joan's lifetime a woman was brought to trial at Lyons (1424) for claiming that she was one of five women sent by God to redeem souls from hell (similar to the self-prophecy of Prous Boneta), and that she could read men's sins on their foreheads. She was tortured, confessed, and was convicted, but was spared the death penalty, perhaps because the papal inquisition was not involved. Her followers, "simple women," continued the life of the sect in remote areas, believing that the person who has achieved tranquility of spirit does not need to observe the canons of the church.[57] We owe this information to Jean Gerson, chancellor of the University of Paris until the English took over the city, the most prominent theologian among the Dauphin's exiled supporters, outspoken puritan, and admirer of Joan of Arc.

It is surprising that Gerson endorsed Joan, for he was deeply skeptical of women prophets. Always ambivalent about mysticism, Gerson placed it above normal rational reflection but at the same time warned of its excesses. Female mystics were not fortunate in the evaluation he made of them: he believed that most of them were weak and unstable, easily seduced by male pseudo-prophets and all too vulnerable to the "Free Spirit" heresy which claimed that the perfect soul can indulge in carnal affections without sin. Gerson was

54. McDonnell, *Beguines and Beghards*, pp. 500-501. Some of the Turlupins fled to Savoy, the rest remained in France but went underground, managing thereby to avoid further persecution.

55. Ibid. The king, Charles V, for example, had put up the money for the persecution of the Turlupins.

56. When two branches of the church came into conflict over the question of the right of appeal, the French parlement asserted its jurisdiction over them both by receiving the following case: in 1403 a woman of Cambrai, Marie Ducanech, prosecuted by the Dominican inquisitor for claiming the right to earn interest on loans, appealed to the archbishop of Rheims. By declaring for her, the parlement asserted the power of an episcopal court over the inquisitional tribunal. Ibid., p. 501, based on Fredericq, *Corpus* 1:261-264, no. 245.

57. Reported by Jean Gerson, "De examinatione doctrinarum" in *Oeuvres complèts*, 1:19-20.

particularly scathing against a certain Mary of Valenciennes and an unnamed woman, both prophets and miracle workers, who claimed that their spirits had been annihilated in the contemplation of God.[58]

But in 1429, in the very weeks before Joan's victory at Orléans and shortly before Gerson's death, he defended her in a treatise in which he praised her for her modesty, declaring that while women ordinarily should not dress as men, she had divine permission to do so.[59] Had not she, a young girl, procured the loyalty and trust of the war leaders? Had she not rallied the French and frightened the enemy? Some prophets were false, but her selflessness proved that God was on her side. The results were miracle enough for Gerson. This tautological reasoning proceeded from his desire to condemn most female mystics while making of the triumphant Joan a brilliant exception. In this sense Gerson is a progenitor of much of the adulatory literature about Joan that has poured forth in the nineteenth and twentieth centuries to exalt Joan the patriotic saint, while conveniently forgetting the great number of female visionaries, prophets, and heretics to whose type she belongs.

***

Joan lived in an age of mysticism, "in which the supernatural was waiting round every corner."[60] The long line of mystics and visionaries whom we have considered are only the French, and only the female, representatives of a European phenomenon. It is readily understandable that late medieval religion produced more female adepts than male, given the opportunities for men in an ever-more-active priesthood. Since the twelfth century, when the doctrine of transubstantiation empowered priests to perform the eucharistic miracle, men had available to them a ready-made, institutionally guaranteed role as miracle worker. And yet, women were as caught

58. For a speculation that Mary of Valenciennes was really Marguerite Porete, see Romana Guarnieri, *Archivio Italiano per la storia della pietà* 5 (1968):453-454, 461-462. The views that Gerson quotes are indeed close to some of Marguerite's statements in *A Mirror for Simple Souls*. For a discussion of Gerson's view of female mystics, see J. Huizinga, *The Waning of the Middle Ages* (New York: Anchor Books, 1954), pp. 196-197.

59. Gerson, "De quadam Puella," trans. in my Appendix. On Gerson's authorship of this treatise, see Dorothy G. Wayman, "The Chancellor and Jeanne d'Arc," *Franciscan Studies* 17 (nos. 2-3, June-September 1957):273-305, where the Latin version of the tract is reprinted.

60. Lucien Fabre, *Joan of Arc*, trans. Gerard Hopkins (London: McGraw-Hill, 1954), p. 10.

up as men in the intense, emotional religious revival of the high middle ages, of which the doctrine of transubstantiation was one part. Their response to this more magical priesthood, which they could not join, was an unprecedented outpouring of visions, prophecies, and healings, in which they saw themselves as fully worthy of the highest calling.

We have seen that women envisioned themselves or other females as saviors or messiahs, as advisors to kings and popes, even as priests and cardinals, or as the holder of the papal office itself.[61] Given this tradition, it is not surprising that Joan believed that the Lord spoke to her, singling her out for a mission which no one else could perform, that she felt herself called to advise the Dauphin, to lead his army, to stand beside him when he was crowned. Even her incredible claim that her voices called her "Daughter of God" seems almost normal and every-day in comparison to the visions of Prous Boneta. In the dazzling light of these visions, let us look at the most mysterious aspect of what Joan said about her own, namely, her absolute certainty about her call.

From the start, as we have seen, she had expressed unequivocal belief about what she was to do and complete certainty that she was the only person who could do it. Her single-mindedness, not to say monomania, carried the day as much as the fact that she fit a well-prepared role. Her successes at court and on the battlefield only deepened her conviction. We should not be surprised that at the trial she defended her voices with audacity. At the second session when she was badgered to take the oath, Joan shot back that:

> If you were well-informed about me, you would wish to have me out of your hands. I have done nothing except by revelation.[62]

St. Michael himself could not have been more aggressive. Two days later when the prosecutor asked her to describe her voices she abruptly changed the subject and, turning to the presiding judge, lashed out at him:

> You *say* you are my judge. Take care what you are doing; for in truth I am sent by God, and you place yourself in great danger.[63]

61. See n. 53.
62. Murray, p. 9.
63. Ibid., p. 16.

With this second warning, more specific than the first, Joan the mystic inspires Joan the shaman, hurling her authority against her judges, defying them, mere priests and bishops, to move against her, the divinely chosen woman.

By the fifth session Joan was angry enough to utter a curse. Taunted about her voices' failure to deliver her from prison, Joan replied darkly that:

> Those who wish to send me out of the world may well go before me.[64]

This was not one of Joan's successful prophecies, but was no doubt her wish. She had admitted before that she had wished her enemies dead: a Burgundian neighbor's head to be cut off, any English to die who would not leave France.[65] Now she predicted the death of her judges.

When refusing yet again to tell everything she knew about her revelations, Joan gave her strongest reiteration of her faith in them, proclaiming:

> But as firmly as I believe in the Christian faith and that God has redeemed us from the pains of Hell, that Voice had come to me from God and by his command.[66]

Only when she had been in court for two weeks straight did she give a glimpse of the awful loneliness of the mystic, allowing that:

> Even though [some of my own party] do not believe, yet am I sent from God.[67]

Quite an admission to make to her judges, but a warning to them also, that she would not be moved from loyalty to her visions. Until she faced death, Joan appears never to have doubted that God was the source of her revelations, that it was He and not Satan who spoke to her.

Far from being a mere aid or accessory to ambition, visionary instructions were as real to fifteenth-century persons as their bodies. And not only one's own visions but other people's as well. Joan's

---

64. Ibid., p. 41.
65. Ibid., pp. 19, 37.
66. Ibid., p. 17.
67. Ibid., p. 49.

judges believed in her voices every bit as much as Joan did: when they asked her to get more information from the voices, they were not playing games with her but were willing to wait for an answer from the spirit world. Joan not only heard but saw, touched, smelled, and argued with her spectral visitors. And when they would leave her, she would weep and beg to be taken with them. Joan longed for her saints, indeed preferred their company over that of mere humans.

Some say that Joan followed a chimera, pursuing it to her own destruction. Joan would insist that her voices were more real than ordinary reality, wiser than any known counsel, more comforting than the sacraments of the church, and, most important, more powerful than anyone else's magic. In the belief that such a thing was possible, she had the agreement of the pre-modern world.

The period we call modern, the era between the eclipse of folk religion and our own day, has lasted for only two hundred years. For two centuries few of the educated elite in the Western world has believed that there is communication between two worlds, between two spiritual levels of our being. We have declared the hearing of voices to be madness. Whereas today Joan's habit of consulting her "counsel" would brand her as schizophrenic, in her own time at least no one called her mad.

In the fifteenth century the European world which had produced Joan's visions was showing signs of strain, even early indications of disintegration. In that declining civilization, its institutions grew defensive and rigid, trying to maintain themselves through litigation and a punitive treatment of "outsiders." The question became, not can there be voices, but from whence come one's voices. Much was wrong in late medieval Europe, and scapegoats had to be found. The Jews and the Cathars, non-Christians that is, filled the role for a while; then new victims were sought. Increasingly Christians turned on their own, labelling outspoken persons as heretics and female miracle-workers as witches. As we will see, Joan qualified as both. Before turning to the accusations against her and the forces that brought her down, we have to see how her mystical visions engendered magical powers for her to use, powers in which her contemporaries, allies and foes alike, believed, and which, for that reason if no other, were sufficient to make of her a shamanic figure.

Chapter Three
Charismatic Heroes:
Joan as Shaman

shä-man: One who uses mediumistic methods,...who resorts to dreams and visions for help and guidance;...a specialist in the use of supernatural agencies, whether conceived as personal spirits or as an impersonal mysterious power...a healer, priest, or magician.
Columbia Encyclopedia, 2nd ed.
No one [else] in the world...can recover the kingdom of France; there is no succor to be expected save from me...because my Lord wills that I should do it.
Joan at Vaucouleurs, Jan. or Feb., 1429

While Joan did not set herself up as one to perform magic for hire, she did regard herself as a Chosen One endowed with supernatural gifts, and she became for her compatriots a shaman, one, that is, who crossed the barrier between this world and the realm of the spirits to become a source of healing strength and saving knowledge, a magical leader in her people's dark hour. To her enemies, these same abilities of Joan's were seen as dangerous, demonic, and almost invincibly powerful.

We have explored the experiences and qualities that distinguish the shaman. There is the sudden call, often at puberty, that puts one in touch with the spirit world. The chosen one is made ill, or at least suffers from behavior so strange that she becomes alienated from her community. Seeking seclusion, she withdraws from family and society, and is given a mission, gifts with which to carry it out, a new identity, and often a new name. She can now offer to cross the boundary into the spirit world to bring back special knowledge and the power to heal, to restore balance and harmony within the community, and, perhaps most striking, to reinterpret the identity of her people. Finally, unlike the mystic, the shaman must be acknowledged by her group; until they allow her to use her power, it is not effective.

Convincing several people in her locality to believe in her calling was, therefore, Joan's first, crucial step. Why should anyone believe that a peasant girl of about seventeen, illiterate and unexceptional in every way, except perhaps a bit too pious, was chosen by God to save France from the English? And yet Joan convinced her cousin Laxart to take her from her parents' house to Vaucouleurs, her immediate goal. In order to get away, she instructed Laxart to tell her father that she was going to help his wife in her confinement, and Laxart had consented to take part in the lie. Further, he had to take her several times to the governor, de Baudricourt, who twice turned them away with instructions "to take her back to her father's house and box her ears," before agreeing to help.[1]

When Joan's next convert, a man-at-arms of the **Vaucouleurs** garrison, Jean de Nouillonpont, questioned her about her mission, he drew from her an astonishing claim:

...before mid-Lent, I must be with the King—even if I have to wear out my legs up to the knees! No one in the world...can recover the kingdom of France; *there is no succour to be expected save from me* ...because my Lord wills that I should do it.[2]
[Emphasis mine.]

De Nouillonpont's remaining doubt, whether the Lord who instructed her was divine or demonic, being settled [she replied that it was God], he promised to take her to the king, touching her hand in pledge. A second squire reported a similar conversion.

Robert de Baudricourt, that rough and skeptical army captain, was harder to convince. Joan waited, impatient, for weeks, for Robert to make up his mind about her. That he too sensed her power is clear from the following incident: he did not doubt that she was a medium, a conduit, that is, for supernatural communications and acts, but he needed to know *with whom* she communicated, with God or with the Devil. Accompanied by a local priest, Robert went to Joan's lodgings in order to have her exorcised. Bowing before the priest, Joan sharply reminded him that she had already confessed to him, implying that she should not be subjected to exorcism.[3] But these incidents were a warning that she might be suspected of diabolism.

Displaying a typical fifteenth-century fear of Satan, Robert was still not satisfied. It took an amazing act of telepathy, Joan's announcement of the French loss at the Battle of the Herrings near

1. Murray, p. 226. Marot, p. 53.
2. Murray, p. 223.
3. Ibid., p. 227.

Orléans *on the day that it happened,* to convince Robert that whatever Joan was, witch or magical virgin, it was worth a try to send her to the Dauphin. But his words as she left, "Go, go, and let come what may,"[4] reveal that he was never truly converted. Joan had utilized prophecy, clairvoyance, ordinary lies, and cunning–and was on her way to France. Wearing different (male) clothing, her hair cropped short, carrying the arms of the knightly class, calling herself by a new name, La Pucelle, and claiming an exclusive, divine mission, she had prepared a shamanic identity.

As Joan travelled, word of "a maid from Lorraine" apparently spread before her, raising curiousity, hope, skepticism, even belief, as people remembered the prophecy that France would be saved by a virgin from the eastern borderlands.[5] Joan did not shrink from identifying herself with that prophecy. Before leaving Domremy, she had begun to drop hints, to prophesy that God had a special plan for her. Although she told *no one* about her voices, not her parents nor even her parish priest, she did speak cryptically to several of her neighbors. A ploughman about her age recalled at the retrial that:

> one day–the Eve of St. John the Baptist [June 23, 1428]–she said to me: 'Between Coussy and Vaucouleurs there is a young girl who, before the year be gone, will have the King of France consecrated.' And, in truth, the following year the King was crowned at Rheims.[6]

To her cousin Durand Laxart she confided, "Was it not foretold formerly that France should be desolated by a woman and should be restored by a maid?"[7] And the woman with whom she lodged while at Vaucouleurs reported that Joan was more explicit:

> 'Do you not know,' she said, 'the prophecy which says that France, lost by a woman, shall be saved by a maiden from the Marches of Lorraine?' I did indeed remember the prophecy, and remained stupefied.[8]

4. Marot, p. 59.
5. Murray, pp. 223-227.
6. Murray, p. 225.
7. Ibid., p. 226. The woman Joan referred to was Isabel of Bavaria, the queen mother, who, when her husband Charles VI went mad, had scandalized France by having an affair with his brother, Louis of Orleans, and had implied that her son the Dauphin might be illegitimate, that is, the product of this affair. The salvific maid, whose virtue would right this royal sin, was of course Joan herself.
8. Ibid., p. 227.

This legend of an armed virgin coming from Lorraine, widely attributed to Merlin, turned up in various forms in Joan's story; and once she reached Vaucouleurs she did not hesitate to identify herself fully with it.[9] Joan was a diviner, and one who placed herself squarely in the center of her divinations.

The ultimate test, of course, was to convince the Dauphin, but neither he nor Joan ever satisfactorily revealed how she established her credibility with him. Having caught the Dauphin's sympathetic interest, she moved with supreme confidence to win over the Armagnac theologians at Poitiers; when they asked for a sign of her calling, she did not ever consider it necessary to produce one. Her acceptance by the army, including some of the cynical nobles, happened so rapidly that we must assume they were well prepared for, were even looking for, a young, telepathic virgin to lead them.

The Count of Dunois, bastard of Orléans, who fought beside Joan in that first battle, believed that she "was sent by God, and that her behavior in war was a fact divine rather than human." His evidence was that she was able to enter the besieged city because of a sudden change of wind permitting her forces to cross the Loire, because the much stronger English forces did not attack them, because Joan had seen a vision of the late King Louis XI and Charlemagne praying for the safety of the Dauphin and the city, and because Joan kept fighting all day after she was wounded by an arrow in the neck. Dunois concluded by associating Joan with Merlin's prophecy of a salvific virgin who would come from an oak wood.[10]

Many other soldiers gave testimony to Joan's supernatural endurance, her marvelous chastity, and her miraculous prophecies. Enjoying considerable popular support after her victories, she found that people turned to her for healing, considering her touch to be efficacious.

Having already decided that she was the devil's disciple, the English and Burgundians now believed that she was the key to a Satanic conspiracy against them. A preacher from the pro-English University of Paris warned a Parisian congregation that a cult had already grown up around her name: when children brought her

9. The legend was mentioned at her first interrogation at Poitiers, in the three depositions at her retrial mentioned above, and in contemporary literary sources. Christine de Pisan, for example, mentioned this prophecy in her poem about Joan written in July, 1429; see below, p. 77.

10. Murray, pp. 232, 234-236, 241. For a detailed account of Joan's military career, see Frances Gies, *Joan of Arc: The Legend and the Reality*, ch. 6 and 8. Although Gies relies too heavily on Dunois' account and exaggerates Joan's role as strategist, still she makes a case for the crucial role played by Joan's aggressiveness.

lighted candles, she annointed their heads with three drops of melted wax. At St. Denis before her attack on Paris, he went on, she had been sponsor at the baptism of two babies, and already images of her were being venerated. These practices he declared to constitute a cult, which the church strictly prohibited to be dedicated to a living person. Furthermore, Joan was a liar and witch, who had made false predictions and encouraged idolatry.[11]

We know more about these disturbing matters than the anonymous preacher could report: an Armagnac archbishop had in fact ordered prayers to be said for Joan, and people did try to kiss her ring and touch her hand. In a time when it was normal for laity to receive communion once a year, Joan laid herself open to suspicion by requesting the Sacrament every day. Quick to elaborate on this excessive piety, her enemies claimed that she had received the Host twice on Christmas Day, a grave sin. The Bourgeois of Paris averred that Joan claimed "she would produce thunder and other marvels if she liked," had heard her voices at a fairies' well, had jumped from a high tower without hurting herself, and had boasted that she was certain she would go to Paradise.[12]

Many of Joan's actions were used against her, proving how dangerous it had become for a lay person, especially female, to speak out about a revelation or to act on a command which she claimed came from God. Yet the stories which relate Joan to the supernatural are all rooted in experiences common enough in her day. As a young girl she took part in the magical practices of folk religion, a fact which her accusers were quick to use against her. When the judges at her trial sent spies to inquire into her past, they brought back report of a magical tree near Domremy. Joan defended herself by connecting the tree with healing customs which were practised in the rural areas of Europe:

> Not far from Domremy there is a tree that they call 'The Ladies' Tree'–others call it 'The Fairies' Tree'; near by, there is a spring where people sick of the fever come to drink, as I have heard, and to seek water to restore their health.

Well aware that she was treading dangerous ground, Joan then began to hedge:

11. Anonymous sermon in Paris: Noël Valois, "Un nouveau témoinage sur Jeanne d'Arc," *l'Annuaire-bulletin de la société l'histoire de France* 1906 (Paris: 1907).

12. Archbishop Gelu's prayers, Quicherat 5:104-105; Joan's communion requests, Murrary, pp. 218, 281; Bourgeois, pp. 261-262.

I have seen them myself come thus; but I do not know if they were healed. I have heard that the sick, once cured, come to this tree to walk about. It is a beautiful tree, a beech, from which comes the 'beau may' [branches used in May Day games].[13]

Her statement "but I do not know if they were healed" was an attempt to distance herself from the practice of pagan magic. She knew that her inquisitors would have heard about fairy folk; clever enough not to pretend ignorance about what everyone in Domremy surely knew, she nonetheless now chose her words with great care when she admitted that:

I have sometimes been to play with the young girls, to make garlands for Our Lady of Domremy. Often I have heard the old folk–they are not of my lineage–say that the fairies haunt this tree. I have also heard one of my Godmothers...say that she has seen fairies there; whether it be true, I do not know. As for me, I never saw them that I know of....

Mindful of protecting her reputation as a virgin, without being asked, she headed off questions about young folk dancing and courting at the tree:

I have seen the young girls putting garlands on the branches of this tree, and I myself have sometimes put them there with my companions;....I may have danced there formerly, with the other children. I have sung there more than danced.[14]

Joan was careful not to mention that she had her own romance with a young man. But Joan's voices, her call from the spirit world, had intervened, and she had broken off with him. When the young man sued for breach of promise, Joan went to Toul to defend herself. The ecclesiastical judge declared her innocent of having made any promise whatsoever, and, as the plaque beside the cathedral today avers, she was then free to set out on the task of saving her country.[15] She concluded her testimony about the fairies' tree

13. Murray, pp. 20-21.
14. Ibid.
15. The plaque on the wall near the cathedral of Toul states that "En l'an 1428 Jeanne d'Arc, diocesaine de Toul, comparut ici devant l'officialité de l'éveque Henri de Ville, preside par Frederic de Maldemaire, doyen de St. Gengoult, dans un procès matrimonial, qui lui fit un jeune homme de Domremy. Ses juges l'ayant déclarée libre de tout lien, *elle put de ce jour entreprendre la merveilleuse chevauchée et sauver la France*"

by mentioning only that:

> Ever since I knew that it was necessary for me to come in France, I have given myself up as little as possible to these games and distractions. Since I was grown up, I do not remember to have danced there.[16]

Twenty-five years after Joan was put to death, a retrial was held, more to clear the French king's name of association with Joan's witchcraft than to absolve Joan of infamy. Nonetheless, the retrial permitted many witnesses to speak to Joan's good name, and in the process, to provide us with considerable additional information about her. Under oath at Domremy, several of her former neighbors explained further about the Fairy Tree. An elderly farmer reported that:

> This tree is called the Ladies' Tree....On Springs Sunday [Laetare Jerusalem] the boys and girls of Domremy are accustomed to go out under this tree; their mothers make loaves for them and, young men and girls, off they go to celebrate Springs...under this tree. There they sing and dance and come back to the Spring at Rains, eat their bread and drink of its waters, as I have witnessed.[17]

The farmer closed with the significant statement that "Joan went there with the other girls and did all that the others did."[18] Young people danced there in spring and summer and on festival days. The birch-boughs were cut probably for a ceremonial cycle of May, a ritual of quest once common in Lorraine. As we have seen, these were the customs associated with May all over Europe, and they were linked with a popular form of belief which, in the eyes of official Christianity, was very dangerous.

Lest there be any doubt about the church's hostility to the fairy tree and its bucolic pleasures, consider further testimony at Joan's retrial. Jean Morel reported that the fairies no longer visited the place, not since people went there to read the gospel of St. John. Beatrix Estellen made it even clearer, maintaining that the curé himself took a crucifix there each year on the eve of Ascension Day,

(emphasis mine).

16. Murray, p. 21.

17. Regine Pernoud, *Joan of Arc, By Herself and Her Witnesses*, trans. Edward Hyams (New York: Stein and Day, 1966), p. 22.

18. Ibid., pp. 22-23.

and sang the gospel at the tree and at the redcurrants' spring.[19]
The same portion of Scripture was read when crops were planted in
the fields, the prologue to St. John's gospel being considered
magical, a talisman that could ward off lightning, Satan, and evil
spirits. Recognizing the power of this ancient magical place, the
church tried to substitute its own power.[20]

When pressed repeatedly at her trial about the "fairy tree" Joan
said she had heard her voices there, but could not remember what
they had told her. She absolutely dissociated herself from knowledge
of the fairies, as well she might while being interrogated in an inquisitional court. But the fact remains that Joan had sung and danced
there with the rest of the village children, and did all that the others
did. She had heard that there was a mandrake vine growing there,
and everyone knew that a mandrake was a powerful talisman,
capable of deadening pain, arousing sexual desire, increasing wealth,
and overcoming barrenness. But Joan denied that she carried a piece
of the root in her bosom.[21] Whether she was merely answering
prudently, or whether her taste for the miraculous ran more to

19. Murray, p. 214. The comments of Jean Morel and Beatrix Estellen are reminiscent of the lament which Chaucer's Wife of Bath made over how the fairies were
driven out of England:

> But now no man can see the elves, you know.
> For now the so-great charity and prayers
> Of limiters and other holy friars
> That do infest each land and every stream
> As thick as motes are in a bright sunbeam,
> Blessing halls, chambers, kitchens, ladies' bowers,
> Cities and towns and castles and high towers,
> Manors and barns and stables, aye and dairies,
> This causes it that there are now no fairies.
> For where was wont to walk full many an elf,
> Right there walks now the limiter himself
> In noons and afternoons and in mornings,
> Saying his matins and such holy things,
> As he goes round his district in his gown.
> Women may now go safely up and down,
> In every copse or under every tree,
> There is no other incubus than he,
> Who would do them nothing but dishonour.
> – *Canterbury Tales*, trans. J.U. Nicolson (Garden City Publishing
> Co., 1934).

20. Apparently the church failed, for when foundation work was begun on the
basilica at Bois Chenu in the 1880s, it found it necessary to remove the magical fountain. Pierre Marot, *Joan the Good Lorrainer at Domremy* (Colmar: Editions S.A.E.P.,
1981), pp. 41-42, 105.

21. Murray, p. 42.

visions than to talismans, we cannot know, but I believe that Joan's imagination was fired by the fables she heard of spirit creatures, magical healings, and powerful talismans. She grew up believing that spirits, whether her saints or some other voices from the spirit world, were more real, more to be trusted, than the people of this world.

What we do know, from repeated testimony at the retrial, is that she went regularly to a secluded shrine called Notre Dame de Bermont about two miles north of Domremy, there to light candles and to pray to the Virgin. Situated on a hill-top just above the spring associated with an eleventh-century miracle worker, Bermont is a typical sacred high place, hundreds of which were once consecrated to pre-Christian holy persons, then to Christian saints and ultimately to the Virgin. Every Saturday (a day devoted to the Virgin) with girls and boys from Domremy and accompanied by her older sister Catherine, Joan went to this hermitage in the woods, in a clearing by a fountain. Within the chapel was a polychrome wood statue of Our Lady of Bermont, carved in a rustic Rhenish style, holding a smiling child carrying a dove, before which Joan prayed.[22] She went to Bermont so often that one witness allowed that "she was there when her parents thought her with the plough or in the fields...."[23] Joan needed time to herself; remote shrines, out of sight of parental vision, furnished excellent places to contact her voices.

That Joan experienced the typical folk religion of Lorraine, dusted with Christian symbolism but based on its own sources of power, as at the Fairy Tree, stands as a reminder to us that she knew rich sources of magic. Joan's spirituality was formed in the countryside, in the world of nature. It is not surprising that the Bourgeois of Paris believed that she had control over nature, that wild birds came to eat out of her hand as if they were tame, a feat attributed to shamans from ancient times.[24] We are right to associate her with the oak-wood, the magic fountain, and the remote chapel; these places sacred to folk religion inspired her, fed her belief in her own powers in a way that the church services did not. What Joan cherished about the church was not entirely what the church taught its members to live by. While she was orthodox enough in her desire for the Eucharist and confession, Joan loved most her saints and the church bells. Living as she did next door to

---

22. Marot, *Joan the Good Lorrainer*, pp. 106-107. The statue is now in the crypt of the Basilica at Bois Chenu consecrated in 1926 to honor Joan.

23. Murray, p. 214.

24. Bourgeois, pp. 233-234.

the parish church, she heard the bells regularly as a child and later told the court of sitting in her garden hard by the churchyard to listen to them. She always maintained that her voices came to her when the bells were ringing, and she begged the church-warden and, later, the army chaplains to ring the bells for half an hour on end.[25]

The most highly charged and numinous object in folk religion was the human body. We have seen the importance of saints' bones (and hair, nails, bath water, etc.) for healing and for purposes of devotion. Now we must consider the value which Joan's society assigned to a certain type of living body, the virginal female, for it was this aspect of folk magic that Joan incorporated into her persona from the beginning.

Joan remained a virgin because she promised her voices that she would: "The first time that I heard the voice, I promised to keep my virginity for as long as it should please God, and that was at the age of thirteen or thereabouts."[26] Sensible in this as in so many other matters, Joan vowed virginity only so long as it was necessary (i.e., to complete her mission). She showed no inclination toward asceticism, the heroics of perpetual virginity, or a cloistered life. Quite simply, she acknowledged that for her voices to come into her life, something had to go out: she traded the usual social life of a village girl for religious experience. One bargained with God, one expected some give-and-take with the saints to whom one prayed. If Joan expected the voices to continue to speak to her, then she must give them a sign; she must make room in her life for the holy. Remaining uncorrupted sexually was Joan's sign of her obedience to them.

The boys at Domremy might laugh at her, and boys and girls might jeer because she was too pious, praying while they were dancing; but Joan knew that she could not enjoy both a boy friend and her voices. Ever since she knew that she must "come into France," she had "given herself up as little as possible to these games and distractions."

As for her public role, her virginity became essential. Shortly after she arrived in Poitiers, the Dauphin ordered a physical examination of her body. Although declared "a true Maid," she had to submit to a second such exam when the English got hold of her.[27] Everyone knew that the Devil worked through women by seducing them; if the English could prove that Joan had had sexual experience, they could

25. Murray, pp. 16, 149-150, 215, 218, 220, 221.

26. Murray, p. 63. See also Warner, *Joan of Arc*, p. 24. Warner's entire discussion of Joan's virginity is exemplary.

27. Ibid., pp. 309, 205.

adduce the Devil as her partner. But the report of her examiners disappointed them.

For the Armagnacs, the fact that she was a virgin became the central claim in her legend. One of the two squires who accompanied Joan on her first famous journey out into the world, from Lorraine to the Dauphin's court at Chinon, later reported that when "I slept each night beside her...I was in such awe of her that I would not have dared go near her; and I tell you on my oath that I never had any desire of carnal feelings for her."[28] Another squire claimed that although "I was strong, young and vigorous in those days–never, despite sight or contact I had with the Maid, was my body moved to any carnal desire for her, nor were any of her soldiers or squires moved in this way."[29]

These testimonies point not so much to Joan's innocence, although they acknowledge it, as to her power. The soldiers felt awe, an admiring fear, of her magical virginity; they would boast years later of how the sight of her, goddess-like, had won them and inspired them. Joan apparently played up her virginal image, referring to herself as "Jehanne la Pucelle," Joan the virgin. She did not use the ordinary term, "vierge," but chose instead the word that means a transitional state, a time of coming-of-age, a passage into sexual maturity.[30] The term "pucelle" announces: take me seriously, I am not a child; and yet, I am innocent of women's ways. In a tantalizing way Joan presented herself as independent of man, the virgin beholden to no man, neither father, husband, lover, nor priest, yet at the same time as a maid who wept easily and who forbade her solders to swear or to keep their whores. This combination of independent strength and feminine tenderness and virtue is extremely seductive; when we add these qualities to the image of a young woman dressed in armor, charging on horseback through the ranks, we can see why her soldiers were bedazzled.

Virginity was also, of course, eminently practical and in fact the only way in which she could embark on the life promised her in her visions. A pregnant Joan on the battlefield? A married Joan, fleeing an irate husband from town to town? A sexually experienced Joan sleeping among the soldiers? No, she needed her virginal innocence to protect her, as well as to leave her unencumbered for the work she had vowed to do.

28. *The Retrial of Joan of Arc*, ed. Regine Pernoud, trans. J.M. Cohen (London: Methuen, 55), p. 134.

29. Ibid., p. 75.

30. Warner, *Joan of Arc*, pp. 22-23.

She did not make it easy for her contemporaries to size her up, to categorize her, nor is it any easier for us: a woman who is a maid, a female virgin who wears men's clothes, a soldier with an uncorrupted body. Small wonder that her followers idolized her while at the same time one of the enemy described her as "a creature *in the form of* a woman...what it was, God only knows."[31] Joan's body was perceived as a supercharged, miraculous body, and was regarded with awe, as much by theologians at the university as by soldiers on the field of battle.

Joan's own attitude toward her powers was at best ambivalent. After the victory at Orléans, wherever she went crowds pressed in to touch her hand, to kiss her ring. Joan allowed them to do so without encouraging them, but when women at Bourges asked her to bless their rosaries and holy objects, she refused, telling them that her friend's touch would do as much good as her own.[32] When the king's examiners asked her for a sign, Joan replied, "I did not come to give signs; give me soldiers and I will show you signs."[33]

And yet, Joan chose to play up to much that her society associated with magic. When asked why her banner displayed a representation of God holding the world, and her two female saints, Joan assured her judges that these were not random choices but that her saints had instructed her to have it decorated thus, and "to take my banner and to carry it boldly."[34]

Given the medieval belief in the magical efficacy of words, especially of holy names, it is not surprising that Joan's judges questioned her closely on the words embroidered on her banner and inserted at the beginning of her letters, "Jhesus Maria." Unexceptional as they may appear to us, these words were considered to be a potent charm, capable of doing great harm if uttered by a witch. A charismatic preacher who crossed Joan's path several times, the Franciscan Brother Richard, exhorted great crowds in Paris, Troyes, Orléans, and other cities to follow the new cult of the Holy Name of Jesus. After hearing his five-hour sermons, men burned their gambling games and mandrakes and women their finery.[35] Although the cult had been granted approbation in 1427 by Pope Calixtus III, it still smacked too much of mechanical superstition to many theologians, and remained the subject of ardent controversy. Joan is thought to have adopted this devotion, as evidenced by her choice of names on

31. Bourgeois, pp. 263-264.
32. Murray, p. 50.
33. Quicherat, 3:204-205.
34. Murray, pp. 58-59.
35. Bourgeois, pp. 230-232.

her banner.[36]

Her judges were suspicious not only of her banner but also of the ring she wore, asking her why she looked at the ring as she went into battle. Assuring them that she valued it only because her parents had given it to her, she then made them all the more suspicious by claiming that she had touched St. Catherine with it. They charged her with engraving the words "Jhesus Maria" on it, and with signing her letters with a cross, which was blasphemy.

Because images and words were credited with miraculous power, the exact figures on Joan's banner had to be investigated. But it was, above all, her actions which provoked the concern and fear of her judges, and Joan had two models on which to draw in building up an image of her supernatural powers, the local magic worker and the Chosen One who received orders from God. First, the role of the village cunning woman, with her fortune-telling, healing powers, detection of stolen or lost goods, prediction of death and future events, and conjuring up of spirits, furnished Joan with magical abilities familiar to all common people of her time. Arriving at the court of Chinon, for example, she was able to identify the Dauphin out of a crowd of nobles. The course of the next miracle–converting Charles himself–is impossible to trace through Joan's contradictory testimony. The best that can be said about that crucial encounter between the monarch and his ardent follower is that it is of a piece with her visions. When she at last gave the judges an account of her sign to the king, she conjured up an angel; although she did not dare name him, surely it was the archangel Michael she had in mind when she claimed that he:

> came in by the door of the room [Joan's room at Chinon]...walked and touched the earth....I accompanied him and went with him by the staircase to the King's Chamber. The Angel went in first, then myself, and I said to the King: 'Sire, there is your sign; take it.[37]

Bearing a golden crown, the angel handed it to the Archbishop of Rheims (the prelate designated to crown all French monarchs) who gave it to the king. Whether Joan actually envisioned this scene at Chinon or fantasized it later, she must have spoken of it, for Christine de Pisan referred to it in the poem she wrote about Joan a few months later. In any case, here Joan has given us a fabulous

36. Jules de la Martinière, "Frère Richard et Jeanne d'Arc à Orléans, Mars-Juillet 1430," *Le moyen age*, 3e série, 5 (Jan-Mars 1934):189-198. Murray, pp. 91-92.

37. Murray, pp. 70-71. See below, p. 134.

instance of the meeting of two worlds.

Getting full value from this revelation, Joan had the angel conveniently remind Charles that he could have his entire kingdom *if he put Joan to work and gave her soldiers.* And Joan claimed at first that several nobles, and then that several hundred nobles and clergy, had seen this sign.

The story sounds like a dazzling invention, but it may throw light not only on Joan's contact with Charles but on how she formed a visionary experience. She started with what she knew: because she had grown up in a parish church dedicated to St. Remi, first bishop of Rheims, she should have known that the bishop of Rheims always crowned the French monarchs.[38] Pulling together the best facts at her command, Joan inserted her favorite magical sign, an angel, into an updated version of the legend of her parish saint, in which the angel declared that the present bishop of Rheims would hand the Dauphin his rightful crown, in a scene which of course focused on Joan as the indispensable catalyst in these crucial events. I suggest that in pursuing Joan's reports on her visions we keep in mind the formula whereby Joan decides, on the basis of widely-known facts, on a course of action and then "upgrades" the decision by reporting that it was told her by a divine person or spirit.

Joan provided other "miracles" early on in her career. Although de Baudricourt had given her a sword when he provided her with men's clothes, armor, and a horse, Joan offered proof of her clairvoyance by sending for a second sword, which she claimed would be found at the chapel of St. Catherine of Fierbois. And of course it was. That Joan had stopped at this shrine only the day before her entry into Chinon, attending three masses there, goes far toward explaining how she knew that a rusty sword lay half buried in the ground behind the altar. But Joan insisted, "I knew by my Voice where it was."[39]

Like most shrines, Fierbois was steeped in legend. It was said that Charles Martel had left his sword there after his crucial victory over the Saracens,[40] and that St. Catherine had miraculously released many French and Scots from English dungeons, freeing them from death sentences, their chains mysteriously falling off.[41] This saint

38. Marot, p. 6. She would have known the ancient story in which Remi baptized Clovis, first king of the Franks, thus assuring that the Frankish people would become Christian.

39. Murray, pp. 28-30.

40. Murray, p. 27, n. 1.

41. Andrew Lang, *The Miracle of Mme. St. Katherine of Fierbois*, trans. from ed. of Abbé J.J. Bourassé, of 1858 (Chicago: Way and Williams, 1897). Another shrine

was Joan's St. Catherine; how appropriate that the sword which Joan carried through all her victories was found, Excalibur-like, covered with ancient rust, embedded in the ground behind Catherine's altar. And how astonishingly effective was Joan at building up her own legend!

When wounded in her first battle by an arrow that penetrated her shoulder for several inches, a wound which she had predicted, Joan returned to battle in a matter of minutes.[42] With these proofs of her clairvoyance, prophetic fulfillment, and magical body, it is small wonder that the French came to think of her as invulnerable, whereas at the sight of her the English trembled with terror and English soldiers, after hearing of her victories, refused to sail for France.

Probably the main role of the spiritually gifted person in folk religion, however, was as healer, and Joan did not fail to qualify there. When she was just beginning public life, Joan denied that she had the gift of healing. The Duke of Lorraine, hearing about her while she was at Vaucouleurs, had asked her to visit him. Suffering from a serious illness, he no doubt assumed that a virginal prophetess would be able to heal. Making the journey to his capital at Nancy, Joan found herself farther from home and in more august company than she had yet been. Showing herself fully equal to this challenge, she assured the duke that she knew nothing of healing, but that he must give up his mistress (by whom he had had five bastards) and take back his wife. Joan had gone to preaching to her betters. But keeping her eye on her goal, she bargained with the old duke: "I said that he should give me his son and some men to take me into France and that I would pray to God for his health."[43] Not yet a miracle worker, Joan was already an aggressive negotiator on her own behalf. Clearly, she was ready to take on the king himself.

After Joan had been accepted by the king, had won a number of victories, and become a heroine to the Armagnacs, she gained confidence in her powers as a thaumaturge. She described her one attempt at public healing thus:

---

connected with miraculous escapes of prisoners was that of St. Foy (St. Faith) at Conques; see Benedicta Ward, *Miracles and the Medieval Mind* (Philadelphia: University of Pennsylvania Press, 1982), pp. 38-39.

42. Pernoud, *Retrial*, pp. 106-107.

43. Pernoud, *Joan of Arc*, p. 38. Joan was referring to the duke's son-in-law, René d'Anjou, ruler of Bar, brother-in-law and life-long friend of Charles VII.

The child was three days old. It was brought before the image of Our Lady. They told me that the young girls of the village were before this image, and that I might wish to go also and pray God and our Lady to give life to this infant. I went and prayed with them. At last, life returned to the child, who yawned three times, and was then baptized; soon after, it died, and was buried in consecrated ground. It was three days, they said, since life had departed from the child; it was as black as my coat; when it yawned, the colour began to return to it. I was with the maidens, praying on my knees.[44]

A dramatic use indeed of the power of virginity, for to the efforts of the young girls, who had marched in procession through the village, Joan added the touch of her body, as she held the infant at the baptismal font. Her judges, however, were, not impressed by the story, but interpreted it as proof of her spiritual arrogance.

Here Joan had moved fully into the role of the miracle worker. Her most audacious claims, however, were in the area of popular messianism. Joan did not shrink from claiming that she was indispensable, that she alone could save France. High as was her respect and love for her king, Joan placed herself in the center of the story; it was she who would carry out the crucial action. She was the instigator, the necessary catalyst in this salvific drama. We have seen how she assured the squire whom she converted at Vaucouleurs that "there is no succor to be expected save from me." She told him further that "what I am commanded to do I will do; my brothers in Paradise have told me how to act....My Lord–that is, God–told me that I must go and fight in order to regain the kingdom of France."[45] To the man with whom she lodged in Vaucouleurs she claimed emphatically that:

I fear them not, I have a sure road: if the enemy are on my road, I have God with me, who knows how to prepare the way to the Lord Dauphin. *I was born to do this.*[46] [Emphasis mine.]

Here she expresses the shamanistic call, the absolute certainty typical of the person who has experienced the mystic vision. By magical acts–recognizing the Dauphin, gaining his support, finding a hidden sword, identifying herself as the fulfillment of the prophecy

44. Murray, p. 52.
45. Ibid., pp. 223-224.
46. Ibid., p. 228.

of a virgin savior, engaging in healing, claiming that God instructed her in all her decisions, constantly referring to her voices–Joan deliberately built up the image of herself as a special person chosen by God.

Some of these abilities were common to magic workers of her time; what is extraordinary about Joan is the extent to which her visions were filled with political content. Unlike many apparitions, her voices did not give her messages for ordinary folk but rather aimed themselves at captains, dukes, kings.[47] It was not that she ever turned against her own class or against the very poor. She was proud that "poor folk came to me readily, because I never did them any unkindness: on the contrary, I loved to help them."[48] But from Vaucouleurs on, she identified herself with her mission, and that mission was to the court of France.[49]

***

In projecting herself into the center of political power through the medium of visionary experience, Joan had ample models to guide her. Although she was by far the most famous visionary of her age, she was not unique: political prophets were numerous, all of them lay and most of them women. As early as the 1270s the French king Philip III had called on several clairvoyant lay women for help, who were described as persons who could tell things past and future and probe secret matters while leading a good life.[50] But when in 1304 Philip IV turned for advice to a beguine, she was accused of attempted murder, interrogated while the soles of her feet were

47. One piece of evidence that detracts from the popular view of Joan as a simple peasant who was "of the people," is that Joan lived out her active life in the company of the nobles of the court and army, and the well-to-do bourgeoisie with whom she stayed in towns. She leased a house in Orléans and never returned to Domremy. And when Joan began wearing armor, she assumed a further identification with the upper class, for by law only they could wear armor.

48. Murray, p. 50.

49. Ibid., p. 59. Joan did not load herself with honors, airs, or wealth. It was to her brothers that the king awarded a coat of arms for the D'Arc family; Joan never used it on her banner, reserving it for religious symbols, and she allowed that "the ten or twelve thousand" she was worth at the time of her capture was "not much treasure to carry on war, very little indeed."

50. McDonnell, *Beguines and Beghards*, pp. 330-332 and pp. 450-452, with the Latin and French texts. Philip III had been desperate to learn whether his wife was guilty of poisoning his son. A different estimate of the clairvoyant women shows a strong ambivalence toward them, calling them *pseudoprophetae*, persons "not approved by any religion."

burned, and imprisoned for a long time.[51] In comparing these two uses of female prophets at the French court, Robert Lerner concludes that "it was safer to have a reputation for the occult in the thirteenth century than in the fourteenth."[52] A contemporary reference to the beguine as a *pseudomulier* was also made against Marguerite Porete; its implication of sexual deviance also hangs over the later accusation that Joan of Arc was "a creature in the form of a woman, whom they called the Maid–what it was, God only knows."[53]

Whatever the hazards, the number of female visionaries who concerned themselves with politics increased in the late 1300s. They were responding to twin evils: the weakening of French royal power by the English invasion and French treachery, and the split in the church, the "Great Schism" caused by the simultaneous election of two popes in 1378, one in Avignon, one in Rome.

Some of the characteristics of the first prophetess to appear will already be familiar to us. Constance de Rabastens, a widow from the region of Albi, had visions in which Christ appeared, encouraging her to interpret Scripture and to spread the message he gave her.[54] It was of course against canon law for lay men and all women to preach, but Constance, like Marguerite Porete, considered that the authority given her direct from God could transcend the canons. Believing that the pope at Rome, Urban VI, was the true pope, she longed for the French people to be on his side. Despondent over the conflicts of the Hundred Year's War, she turned to the count of Foix, a partisan of Charles VI, to stand against the pro-English nobles. In the best apocalyptic tradition, she united these two concerns by prophesying that the count would establish Urban VI in his full power, and then lead the kings of Western Europe to the conquest of the Holy Land. For her efforts, in 1385 Constance was taken in chains to the inquisitor of Toulouse, forbidden to publish her visions, and imprisoned. We know nothing more of her fate.

The prophecies of another female visionary offer further proof of the anguish caused by the papal schism. The widow Jeanne-Marie de Maillé, a recluse in a hermitage beside a Franciscan monastery at Tours, prophesied in 1396 the election of a Franciscan pope who

51. The Continuator of the Chronicle of Nangis, *Recueil des historiens des Gaules et de la France*, ed. Bouquet, 20:590.

52. Lerner, *The Heresy of the Free Spirit*, 70 ff.

53. Bourgeois, p. 240.

54. The material on Constance de Rabastens is taken from André Vauchez, "Les Soeurs de Jeanne," *Le Monde* (6 January 1980):15, based on a Catalan version of Constance's confessions edited by Noël Valois.

would end the Schism, a prediction fulfilled in the papal election of 1409.[55] Despite her hermit's life she took deep interest in the political troubles of the day, spending long hours in private conversation with Charles VI when he visited Tours. Moved by the deepening crisis caused by the king's madness, in 1398 Jeanne-Marie left her seclusion, went to Paris and advised the king again of the message she had for him from God; unfortunately we do not know the substance. We do know what she said to Queen Isabelle, now under the suasion, and rumored to be the mistress, of the king's brother, Louis, Duke of Orléans. Jeanne-Marie reproached Isabelle for her misconduct and for the luxury of her court, especially inappropriate in a time when taxes were high and people were suffering the depredations of the plundering Free Companies. Luckier than some prophets, Jeanne-Marie ended her days peacefully in her hermitage in Tours, perhaps because she was protected by the Franciscans with whom she lived and who must surely have approved of her papal prophecies.

A more dramatic and disturbing case is that of Marie Robine (Marie of Gascony or Avignon), a simple peasant woman who came on pilgrimage to Avignon in 1387, seeking healing for an illness.[56] Miraculously cured at the tomb of a cardinal, she settled as a recluse in the Cemetery St. Michael, living on alms given her by the popes, first Clement VII and, after 1394, Benedict XIII. In order to end the Schism, France, England, and Spain sent an embassy in 1397 to each of the papal curias, in Avignon and in Rome. At about this time Marie began to have visions which gave her instructions for the French monarchy about the Schism. At the peak of this turmoil Marie travelled to Paris, tried vainly to talk with Charles VI but did manage an interview with Queen Isabelle in which she prophesied that the Avignon pope, Benedict XIII, should resign. And that did in fact become the policy: France tried the bold step of withdrawing obedience from the Avignon pope, an action which threw the French church into a crisis and eventually caused the French to settle for neutrality.[57]

55. Ibid. See also Donald Weinstein and Rudolph M. Bell, *Saints and Society: The Two Worlds of Western Christendom, 1000-1700* (Chicago, 1982), p. 94. I regret that this work was not published in time to be used more fully, for its analysis of gender in sainthood elucidates some of Joan of Arc's problems. For background on the Schism, see *History of the Church*, ed. H. Jedin and J. Dolan, 4:401-417.

56. Noël Valois, "Jeanne d'Arc et la prophétie de Marie Robine," *Mélanges Paul Fabre* (Paris, 1902), based on Marie's unedited *Livre des visions et des révélations*, and on the reported words of Master Jean Erault at Joan's retrial (cf. Murray, pp. 269-270). For the purported prophecy itself, see Quicherat 3:83-84.

When Marie returned to Avignon, her visions continued but became more pessimistic and apocalyptic. Believing that France would be ravaged by the Antichrist, she reported this radical vision: God told her that since the King of France had done nothing to restore the condition of the church militant to unity, "we will depose him from his throne by the means of his subjects, and many will die in rivers of blood, and one will say, 'Here was Paris!'" These were revolutionary words, which Marie was wise not to utter while she was in the capitol itself.[58]

One of Joan's examiners at Poitiers, Master Jean Erault, described a vision reported to him by Marie Robine. Marie had seen a vast amount of armor, and fearing that she was intended to wear it, she protested that she could not be a warrior. She was assured "that the armor was not for her but that a maiden who should come afterwards should bear these arms and deliver the kingdom of France from the enemy." And Jean Erault had believed fervently that Joan was the maiden of whom Marie prophesied.[59]

All three of these visionaries were in the tradition of two more famous women, the nuns Catherine of Siena and Bridget of Sweden, who a generation earlier had struggled to bring about the return of the papacy to Rome from its long "captivity" in Avignon at the hands of the French monarchs. Receiving prophetic visions, they had addressed their views to popes, kings, and the nobility of Europe and had become famous. Both had the protection of convent life. Widow of a nobleman, Bridget was able to found her own order,[60] and Catherine was a Dominican tertiary, whose disciple, Raymond of Capua, wrote her biography and became Master General of the Dominican Order.[61] Bridget became a saint in 1391 and Catherine in 1461, indicating the advantages, both in this life and the next, of membership in an order.

As we have seen, in Joan's own time the well-known visionary nun St. Colette also received the confidence of the nobility, being consulted for over forty years by the mother of the duke of Burgundy and employed during the Schism as negotiator with her patron the antipope Felix V.[62] Another lay female prophet, a woman

57. Denys Hay, *Europe in the Fourteenth and Fifteenth Centuries* (New York: Holt, Rinehart & Winston, 1966), p. 282.

58. Vauchez, "Les Soeurs de Jeanne," my translation.

59. Murray, pp. 269-270.

60. Hay, *Europe in the Fourteenth and Fifteenth Centuries*, pp. 315-316.

61. *ODS*, pp. 70-71.

62. *Vita Sanctae Coletae (1381-1447)*, ed. Yves Cozaux, et al. (Leiden: Brill, 1982), pp. 141-143; *NCE* p. 3; Murray, pp. 52-53.

whom Joan clearly looked upon as a competitor and whom she tried to vanquish from the scene, was Catherine de la Rochelle, a visionary working with Brother Richard, who met Joan in the fall of 1429. Joan's string of victories had ended in September with her failed attack on Paris, and she was trying to raise money to hire more men-at-arms. Catherine's apparition, "a white lady dressed in cloth-of-gold," had instructed her to go to the towns loyal to Charles and to demand the people's silver and treasure; if any held out, she would have the gift of knowing and of discovering the treasure (the adept's gift of finding lost or concealed objects). With this wealth she would hire soldiers for Joan. Joan's reply to this offer of help must be read in her own words:

> I told Catherine that she should return to her husband, look after her home, and bring up her children.[63]

There was no room in Joan's mission for a second miracle-worker. There certainly wasn't room for a married woman, one who had not bothered to dedicate her virginity to the success of her mission.

Joan of course checked with her voice, who confirmed her opinion by declaring that Catherine's mission was "mere folly and nothing else." Joan promptly wrote this piece of information to the king, and reminded him of it again when she next saw him.

For once not content with her heavenly counsel, Joan carried out her own test of Catherine's authenticity as a diviner; she would sleep with Catherine in her bed one night, in order to see the "white lady" herself. Unable to stay awake the first night, Joan was told that she had missed her. Undaunted, Joan took a nap the next day and tried again. That night, although Joan kept the vigil, she saw nothing, proof enough that Catherine was a fraud. Had not the king, and many others, seen Joan's Angel when he appeared with her at Chinon?

Despite Joan's rejection of her, Catherine generously gave her sound advice: not to attack La Charité-sur-Loire, because the weather had turned too cold. Joan let herself be persuaded otherwise by the nobles, and the attack failed. The two women disagreed on a more fundamental issue, the possibility of peace negotiations with the Burgundians. When Catherine declared she wanted to visit the Duke of Burgundy to make peace, Joan replied bluntly that France's problems would more likely be settled by the lance.

63. Murray, p. 53.

But Joan lost more than money and good advice through her jealousy and discrediting of Catherine. Brother Richard, who believed in Catherine, fell out with Joan over this matter, and Catherine herself understandably turned against Joan. After Joan's capture, she gave evidence to a pro-English court in Paris that Joan had often proclaimed that she had two counsellors whom she called "counsellors of the Fountain," and she warned that if Joan was not well-guarded she would escape from prison by the help of the Devil.[64] Catherine could claim true revenge, for by these words she had indicted Joan twice for witchcraft. Joan's reputation fared better with her other contemporary lay visionary, Pieronne of Brittany, who defended the imprisoned Maid and endured the same death at the stake, for refusing to recant of her claim that she frequently saw God.

Another woman whose life became involved with Joan's memory, but in a scandalous way, Claude des Armoises, is only doubtfully a mystic, but should be mentioned here.[65] Running into trouble with the inquisitor of Cologne over the male attire which God directed her to wear, Claude fled to France, where she was soon in hot water with the church again for having hit her mother, an offense so grievous that she was required to atone by a visit to the pope. Once in Italy, however, she reverted to form, dressed as a man, fought as a soldier in the pope's army, and killed two men. On her return to France c. 1440 she was taken up by Joan's two brothers, who sponsored a tour in which they exhibited her *as Joan*, claiming that the Maid had not been killed in the flames of Rouen but had been substituted for at the last minute and was still alive.

Being from Lorraine, herself having had a message from God to wear men's clothing, and being experienced in war, Claude no doubt made a believable stand-in. Welcomed enthusiastically at Orléans and

---

64. Ibid., p. 360. If Catherine's accusation can be trusted, it throws light on Joan's use of her visions: when Catherine claimed that she was in touch with a White Lady, Joan topped her by proclaiming that she had *two* spirits. Further evidence that after joining the army Joan spoke freely, even perhaps boastfully, of her connections with the spirit world, lies in the fact that Christine de Pisan had heard that Joan was guided to the king by an angel (see p. 51).

65. Bourgeois, pp. 337-338; Vauchez, "Les Soeurs de Jeanne." If Claude des Armoises, as described by the Bourgeois, is the same Claude mentioned in Jacob Nider's *Formicarius*, then this incredible woman did indeed have visions, believing that God instructed her to dress as a man. Nider had complained of "women who, dressed in the habit of men, pretend that they were sent by God," and cited a certain Claude, originally of the diocese of Cologne, who took up the life of an army officer, was summoned by the inquisitor, but succeeded in fleeing to France. For Nider's posthumous attack on Joan, see Quicherat 4:502-504.

elsewhere in the provinces, she ran into trouble as she approached
Paris. The English-controlled University and Parlement sent soldiers
to arrest her. She was exposed as a married woman with two sons,
but was let off. Turning soldier again, she joined the garrison at
Paris. After that, we know no more. Had Claude been in conscious
competition with Joan? Had she too known of the legend that an
armed woman would save France, a maiden from Lorraine? Claude
was no virgin, but she may have been inspired by some of the same
sources and heard the same divine command about male clothing as
Joan.

The custom whereby royalty consults divinely favored seers is at
least as ancient as King Saul's visit to the Witch of Endor, and as
recent as President Lyndon Johnson's turning to two Franciscan
friars.[66] Although in Joan's time women predominated in this role,
we find the male hermit of St.-Claude, Jean de Gand, at the French
court in 1421. Jean had received a message from heaven, instructing
him to go to the leaders of both sides in the war, to the Dauphin
and to Henry V, to convince them to lay down their arms. This
peace-making vision, so different from Joan's later command to drive
the English out of France, apparently appealed to Charles, who
invited the hermit to his court several times. He managed also to
speak twice to Henry V, but failed to negotiate the peace treaty that
he desired. Because he predicted that Charles would gain the court
of France, the hermit has been seen as a precursor of Joan,[67] but
since he retreated back to his hermitage after making this prophecy,
he scarcely qualifies.

Because he was a man of peace, one wonders what Jean de Gand
thought of the young woman in armor who came upon the scene
eight years later and accomplished the fulfillment of his prophecy. In
truth, he was more the forerunner of the pacifist Catherine de La
Rochelle than of Joan. Although the hermit lived until 1439, we
have no record of his thoughts on these matters.

In addition to utilizing the hermit of St. Claude and Brother
Richard, the Armagnacs promoted a holy man, one William the
Shepherd, whose shamanic gifts were attested to by his stigmata.
Once Joan was captured, the Archbishop of Rheims, never an
unqualified admirer of hers, soon found William and installed "this
poor idiot," as the Bourgeois called him, to be the Armagnac's new

66. I Samuel 28:7-25; *New York Times*, 13 May 1967, 1:7. Afraid that his decision
to bomb Hanoi would trigger World War III, the President visited his "little monks"
at a Roman Catholic church in Washington.

67. R. Jacquin, "Un précurseur de Jeanne d'Arc," *Revue des Deux Mondes* (15 May
1967), pp. 222-226.

mascot. Captured when the French were routed at Beauvais, William was paraded through Paris in the procession honoring the arrival of the nine-year-old English king, Henry VI. Along with tableaux featuring mermaids, wild men, Amazon queens, and "a lily whose buds and flowers spouted out milk and wine for everyone to drink,"[68] William was exhibited bound by ropes. He is believed to have been thrown into the Seine tied in a sack and to have drowned.

***

The question is not why Joan had visions but why or how her visions focused on the crisis in the French monarchy. The Dauphin's desperate plight was of course common knowledge and of common concern, but few Frenchmen, whether of high or low status, claimed to have an answer. Many of the nobles, their fortunes and ranks depleted by a century of warring with England, were by the 1420s sitting it out. The merchant class were by and large cooperating with the English and their Burgundian allies in order for their businesses to survive. Most hard-pressed were the peasantry, heavily taxed, their lands looted by the armies of both sides.

These were times when the French labored to survive, not times to dream about the greatness of the French crown. And yet, Joan did. I believe that there was one source from outside folk religion that might have fired her mind to such dreams. Before we can speculate about this, however, we need to look at the political and military crisis in the French border lands in the ten or so years while Joan was growing up there, her teenaged years when her voices began to speak to her, and to ask what messianic and political prophecies she may have heard. Finally, we can understand her astonishing rise to prominence better by looking at her through the eloquent words of the most famous woman writer of her time, Christine de Pisan.

Since the lands of the Meuse valley in which Domremy is situated were intricately divided by subinfeudation, they were frequently fought over.[69] The area was rendered even more unstable because

68. Bourgeois, p. 266 and n. 1, and p. 269.
69. The following historical summary is based on Marot, *Joan the Good Lorrainer*, pp. 10-17. Most of the land east of the Meuse belonged to the Duke of Lorraine, nominally a liege vassal of the German emperor but in fact an independent agent. Most lands west of the Meuse were claimed by the duchy of Bar or the county of Champagne, nominally loyal to the French crown but in fact independent also. To further confuse the jurisdictions and loyalties, much of the land in both territories still belonged to the great church holdings. The area around Domremy was in the diocese

the French monarchy could claim with certainty only a few walled towns; Vaucouleurs was one. Domremy itself belonged to the duchy of Bar, and hence was "French," but was in the diocese of Toul, and could therefore consider its inhabitants as "Lorrainers." Joan exemplified the confusion perfectly: calling herself a Lorrainer, she developed a passionate loyalty to the king of France and *went into France*, that is, left the Lorraine borderlands to seek the king in his province below the Loire, that central area of France which was all he still controlled.

The treaty of Troyes in 1420, signed when Joan was about eight, had signalled the beginning of the end of French hopes in the area, which gradually fell under English sway.[70] As if these foreign interventions were not sufficiently menacing, the long, bitter war had created an even worse curse: the marauding companies of freebooters, groups of armed men who fought sometimes for the English, sometimes in the pay of the French, other times on their own. Few villages escaped their plundering and murdering. In an attack on Sermaize, for example, Joan's cousin by marriage was shot down in front of the village church. Closer to home, in 1419 an outlaw squire who had ravaged the Meuse valley captured thirty-three men in a battle just two kilometers from Domremy. In an agreement signed by Joan's father Jacques d'Arc, the inhabitants of Domremy were forced to put themselves under the squire's protection, at a high price.[71]

As more towns went over to the English, local brigands became more daring. One gang-leader, Henry d'Orly, raided Domremy and the neighboring village, seized the cattle and was making away with them when a few men sent by the lady of Domremy intercepted him, recovered the cattle, and executed the brigand leader.[72] Justice was as harsh as the outlaws whom it punished.

By July 1428 Vaucouleurs, nineteen kilometers north of Domremy, was under siege by Anglo-Burgundian forces. The villages to the south were forced to evacuate. Joan, her family, and many of their neighbors fled to the nearest fortified town, Neufchâteau, a few kilometers to the south, where they took refuge for several weeks. While there, Joan confessed several times to the grey friars at

of Toul in Lorraine, which owned many villages outright.

70. Ibid., p. 18. The French queen, Isabel of Bavaria, in close alliance with the Burgundians, had handed over the realm to the English. Giving her daughter in marriage to the young English King Henry V, she repudiated her own son, the Dauphin.

71. Ibid., pp. 18-21.

72. Ibid., p. 21.

the Franciscan monastery.[73] When the villagers returned, much of Domremy including the church had been burned.[74]

All of these horrors, including the constant fear of attack, became part of the daily life of the villagers, shaping the minds of the children as a wartime childhood always does. In a manner little different from the hostility expressed today by children in Beirut or Belfast, the youngsters of Domremy and the nearby Burgundian village of Maxey squared off, acting out the hatreds of which they heard their parents speak. Joan recalled that:

> As soon as I knew that my Voices were for the King of France, I loved the Burgundians no more. The Burgundians will have war unless they do what they ought; I know it by my Voice. The English were already in France when my Voices began to come to me. I do not remember being with the children of Domremy when they went to fight against those of Maxey for the French side; but I certainly saw the Domremy children who had fought with those of Maxey coming back many times, wounded and bleeding.

> Judge: Had you in your youth any intention of fighting the Burgundians?

> Joan: I had a great will and desire that my King should have his own Kingdom.[75]

Part of the pressure that war placed on young people was the need for greater surveillance by their parents. Joan told her judges that "my mother told me many times that my father had spoken of having dreamed that I, Jeanette, his daughter, went away with the men-at-arms. My father and mother took great care to keep me safe, and held me much in subjection." Such discipline would be galling to any teenager, but to one attempting to slip away to save her country, it must have been excruciating. The pressure was severe on both generations. Joan's father told her brothers that if Joan should go off with soldiers, "if this thing would happen that I have dreamed about my daughter, I would wish you to drown her; and if you would not do it, I would drown her myself." And Joan confessed, "He nearly lost his senses when I went to Vaucouleurs."[76]

73. Murray, pp. 9-10.
74. Marot, p. 50.
75. Ibid., p. 19.

That Jacques d'Arc had these dreams after Joan began to hear her voices indicates that he suspected something. Was she dropping hints about her plans? Or was her behavior so odd that he guessed that *something* was afoot, and out of paternal anxiety assumed that she was attracted to soldiers? Perhaps she merely showed an unusual interest in military and political news. More likely, the time she spent listening to her voices had affected her personality; the shaman, we recall, is forced outside her community and appears odd or ill.

She reported that in the summer of 1428 her visions increased, urging her more insistently to take action, to carry out what they had long advised her to do. When the English besieged Orléans, the Dauphin's last stronghold north of the Loire, in October of that year, it seemed to those loyal to the Dauphin that the end had come. By January of 1429 Joan had made her way to Vaucouleurs and made public her mission.

***

This dramatic backdrop of civil war and foreign invasion might fire any young person's mind. What projected Joan's natural concern for her country into an epic vision of its redemption through her military inspiration is still unanswered. Joan's dreams were on an heroic scale, not an unknown phenomenon among teenagers, to be sure, but extravagant for a young girl in any patriarchal culture, and wildly presumptuous for a poor peasant of either sex. Both class and gender worked against her, but they seem not to have given her pause. *Somewhere*, from *someone*, Joan had heard tales, had sampled legends, that gave her the kernel of her plot.

That someone may have been a person, lay or cleric, familiar with the political prophecies of several radical French Franciscans. It would not be necessary for Joan's informants to have read any of the apocalyptic literature, for it had been widely disseminated for well over a century, had found its way into sermons and into many a quasi-heretical discussion in which extreme solutions were sought for the problems of the French people. Of the considerable literature on which these ideas were based, several tracts bear looking at for what they suggest about visions of the French king.

A radical French Franciscan of the mid-fourteenth century, Jean de Roquetaillade, whose mind was receptive to visions and prophecies was much influenced by the millenarian visions of the twelfth-century abbot Joachim of Fiore.[77] Roquetaillade looked at the

76. Ibid., pp. 64-65.

European political situation with an Iron Curtain mentality: he saw the bad German emperor allied with the bad (that is orthodox) Franciscans versus the "true pope" (a figure who unfortuntely remains outside of history), his allies the radical ("Spiritual," later "Observant") Franciscans–and the catalyst of the good guys, the King of France. For his efforts in producing these prophecies, Roquetaillade spent many years in Franciscan and papal prisons, but his ideas were not entirely discredited. In his mature work the role of the French king has become pivotal: he is "the temporal instrument through whom God will bring in the final age of Beatitude." He will be elected Roman Emperor, will destroy Islam, subdue the Turks, convert the Jews, and, in league with the Angelic Pope and the radical or pure Franciscans, he will rule the entire world from Jerusalem.

This glorification of the French monarch was taken up by the Italian Telesphorus, who wrote of a cosmic conflict between the forces of Anti-Christ (the German emperor and a German pseudo-pope) and those of the Angelic Popes and the French king, who will be named Charles. After destroying all the forces of Anti-Christ, they will recover the Holy Land in a last, great Crusade and will bind Satan for a thousand years. Many, many manuscripts of this work circulated, the most popular of which hailed the "Second Charlemagne," Charles the son of Charles from the nation of the Lily, who after putting down internal rebellions would conquer all of Europe and Jerusalem.[78]

Of the numerous copies of this prophecy known, the one dedicated to young Charles VI of France (the Dauphin Charles' father) concerns us most. Added to the revolutionary writings known as the *Vaticinia*, emanating from Italy probably early in the fourteenth century, these prophecies offer a script in which the French King, the *rex generosus* of Pepin's line, sets all political scores right, is crowned Emperor–and then rules the world with a second Angelic Pope who is, of course, French also.

Marjorie Reeves makes the perceptive comment that these radical political prophecies "evolved only as ardent visionaries, such as the

---

77. Marjorie Reeves, *Joachim of Fiore and the Prophetic Future* (New York: Harper & Row, 1976), pp. 66-82. The following passage is based on Reeves' work.

78. Ibid., p. 70. The "Second Charlemagne's" career would encompass "the destruction of all tyrants in his own kingdom and carry him triumphantly through the subjugation of western Europe, the destruction of Rome and Florence, the conquest of Greece and the eastern nations, until he reaches Jerusalem. The divine arm will be always with him and no one will be able to resist him."

Spiritual Franciscans, were pressed into an impossible dilemma by the attempt to hold together two incompatible principles: obedience to the papacy and loyalty to their vision."[79] Reeves' point could apply as well to Joan, who wanted to be loyal both to the church and to her visions, who was forced in the end to a terrible choice, but not before her interpretation of her mission had become considerably more radical than when she had started out. Perhaps it is the nature of absolute loyalties to force one into more radical concepts, and into tragic choices.

These fourteenth-century Franciscan visions were radical to the point of being revolutionary. Joan had early developed a far-reaching, indeed revolutionary ideal of her own: before she had even taken the field, she sent a letter to the English besieging Orléans, challenging them to withdraw from France and then to join the French in a crusade. Alluding to this project again on the day that Charles was crowned, Joan inspired the belief in court circles that she had promised Charles the conquest of the Holy Land. And she apparently also threatened the heretical Hussites that she would "turn against you, to extirpate the dreadful superstition with my blade of iron."[80] Joan's vision of the French king as the central figure in the reordering, the right-ordering of the world thus apparently included her participation in the freeing of the Holy Land. For a challenge so large she needed an image of the monarch which rendered him perfect (she never criticized Charles, not even when he forsook her) and invincible (she never considered that he and she would not win). In the dramatic script written by the millenarian Franciscans, in whatever portion or form of it she may have heard, Joan could have found the larger-than-life, magical portrait of her Second Charlemagne.

Where could she have come across such ideas? An obvious source would have been the Franciscans at Neufchâteau to whom she confessed; heterodox ideas often found their way into otherwise orthodox minds. Given the extremity of the times, in that summer of

79. Ibid., p. 78.

80. Joan's letter to the English, Murray, pp. 36-38. The language, which Joan proudly affirmed that she dictated, is bellicose and arrogant: "...give up to the Maid, who is sent hither by God, the King of Heaven....King of England, I am a chieftan of war [Joan denied having made that claim] and if this be not done, wheresoever I find your followers in France, I will make them leave, willingly or unwillingly; if they will not obey, I will have them put to death." Harsh words from the girl who had come from Vaucouleurs only three or four weeks earlier. The letters on coronation day, Tisset-Lanhers 2:185-187; and to the Hussites (Joan's authorship is disputed), Quicherat 5:156-159.

1428, even perfectly orthodox friars may have been drawn to discussing radical solutions. But one need not look only to the Franciscans. Joachite radicalism had been in circulation in Europe for over two hundred years, frequently condemned but never driven out. Any wandering preacher or theologically minded lay person could pick up these ideas and pass them on. It is believed that Joan's mother had gone on pilgrimage to Le Puy (hence her last name of Romée, given to persons who had been pilgrims), one of the most ancient holy sites, one of the places vouchsafed an epiphany of the Black Virgin; there she might have heard more than the usual sermonic fare served up at Domremy.

Some literature current at the time also carried grand visions of the French crown. Popular poets emphasized the divine origin and destiny of France and predicted that it was God's will that France would triumph over her enemies. The monarch and the Virgin Mary were seen as the chosen agents of national redemption. And even as Joan was making her name at Orléans, writers were at work creating a legend about her, adapting the anonymous prophecy "O insigne lilium," which incorporates the Second Charlemagne theme, by transferring the role of Mary to Joan herself. Charles's propagandists also rewrote the Merlin prophecy in order to name Joan as the miraculous virgin. Among the theologians, Archbishop Gelu of Embrun and, as we have seen, the preeminent French scholar of the day, Jean Gerson, wrote tracts in the spring of 1429 affirming that Joan was indeed a second Deborah, the salvific virgin long prophesied.[81]

The air in France was full of prophecies and expectations of a miraculous female saviour; these beliefs could have fed Joan's imagination before she came to France, and almost certainly magnified her vision of herself in the weeks immediately after she arrived at court. As Deborah Fraioli concluded after an intensive study of prophetic literature relating to Joan, "the existence [of this literature] is a caution against the dogmatism of those who insist on the singular insight and utter originality of Joan, or of those who would deny any relationship between the content of Joan's voices and the temper of the times....Joan was at least as much a creature of her time as she has previously been declared to be separate from it."[82] The extravagant, desperate nature of the Franciscans' solutions to the problems of their late medieval world are of a piece with the

81. Deborah Fraioli, "The Literary Image of Joan of Arc: Prior Influences," *Speculum* 56, no. 4 (October 1981):811-830.

82. Ibid., p. 828.

fabulous, desperate dream of Joan.

***

These same Franciscan prophecies can be found in an extraordinary poem composed in praise of Joan. Writing in the days immediately following the crowning of Charles at Rheims (the exact coronation date, July 17, 1429, is mentioned in the poem), the foremost woman writer in France, Christine de Pisan, penned a resounding war-poem in celebration of Joan's leading the French army to victory at Orléans.[83] Although the poem focuses on "the blessed Maid," it pays great respect to Charles, describing both him and Joan in the superlatives we have found in Franciscan literature:

> And you Charles, King of France, seventh of that noble name, who have been involved in such a great war before things turned out at all well for you, now, thanks be to God, see your honour exalted by the Maid who has laid low your enemies beneath your standard (and this *is* new!).[84]

Developing a prophetic concept, Christine claimed that God had destined Charles to perform great deeds, for:

> there will be a King of France called Charles, son of Charles, who will be supreme ruler over all Kings. Prophecies have given him the name of "The Flying Stag," and many a deed will be accomplished by this conqueror (God has called him to this task) and in the end he will be emperor.[85]

Weaving together the themes of the divinely chosen girl and the magnanimous ruler, Christine wrote that God has decreed that despite the evil of the treacherous English, the miraculous French pair will set the world aright. First, Joan will be the scourge of heretics and schismatics.

---

83. Christine de Pisan, *Ditié de Jehanne D'Arc*, ed. and trans. Angus J. Kennedy and Kenneth Varty (Oxford: Society for the Study of Medieval Languages and Literature, 1977). For an excellent discussion of the *Ditié*, see Deborah Fraioli, "The Literary Image of Joan of Arc: Prior Influences."

84. *Ditié*, p. 42.

85. Ibid., p. 43.

> She will restore harmony in Christendom and the Church. She
> will destroy the unbelievers people talk about, and the heretics
> and their vile ways, for this is the substance of a prophecy that has
> been made....

Joan's show of power will culminate in a joint military venture which
will accomplish what a dozen Crusades have failed to do, to bring
world peace and universal Christian rule.

> She will destroy the Saracens, by conquering the Holy Land. She
> will lead Charles there, whom God preserve! Before he dies he will
> make such a journey....It is there that she is to end her days and
> that both of them are to win glory, there that the whole enter-
> prise will be brought to completion.[86]

Christine's powerful vision of French world conquest, of France as
the avenging arm of God against evil, both local (the English) and
world-wide (non-Christians), is so remarkably like what Telesphorus
had written fifty years before that I assume she had seen his work.

Christine's poem has an additional theme not found in the
Franciscan prophecies. As early as 1399 Christine had entered into a
public debate on the cause of women; as Joan Kelly has pointed out,
Christine produced the first known feminist statement.[87]
Contributing to this debate by her reply to the misogynous writings
of Jean de Meung in the *Romance of the Rose*, Christine was well-
prepared to praise Joan *as a woman*, and she did so with spirit and
ironic humor. Comparing Joan to Moses, Joshua, Gideon, Hector,
and Achilles, she claims that Joan's fame should be greater than
theirs because she is only "a little girl of sixteen."[88] Joan has accomplished more even than Esther, Judith and Deborah, for although
God performed miracles through these women, he has done more
through this Maid, a mere "Pucellette."

The reason for Joan's superiority over all previous heroes and
heroines is that she was called to a greater mission than they. The

---

86. Ibid., p. 47 and n. on p. 70, lines 337-339. Twice Joan had referred to the
possibility that she might organize a crusade, in letters written before Christine
composed the *Ditié* and therefore possibly known to her. See also Maurice Chaume,
"Une Prophétie relative à Charles VI," *Revue de moyen âge Latin* 3 (1947) for a discussion of other royal saviour prophecies (pp. 27-42) and mention of Joan's crusading
ambitions (p. 36).

87. Joan Kelly, "Early Feminist Theory and the 'Querelle des Femmes,'
1400-1789," *Signs: Journal of Women in Culture & Society* 8.1 (Autumn 1982):4-28.

88. This and the following quotations are taken from the *Ditié*, pp. 42-46.

saving of France exceeds delivering the Israelites from their various oppressions or conquering Troy. Since Christine's patriotism for her adopted country knew no limits, its saviors, therefore, must be the ultimate miracle-workers.

In order to portray Joan in this messianic role, Christine stresses how God chose her:

> Blessed be He who created you, Joan, who were born at a propitious hour! Maiden sent from God, into whom the Holy Spirit poured His great grace.

The Marian overtones of this language were picked up by other fifteenth-century Frenchmen, including Matthieu Thomassin who had reprinted Christine's *Ditié* about Joan in 1456, writing that Joan was the most miraculous sign of love that God had shown to the King. Thomassin maintained that all Christianity was blessed through two women, the Virgin Mary and Joan, and concluded that while "la pucelle vierge Marie" had made atonement for the entire human race, "ladicte pucelle Jehanne" had atoned for and restored the kingdom of France.[89] Identification with the Blessed Virgin was one more reward for Joan's virginity.

Emphasizing again the foreordained nature of Joan's calling, Christine added that "Never did Providence refuse you any request. Who can ever begin to repay you?" The prophetic irony of that last line could not have been intended by Christine, but she played on historical fact when she wrote that Joan "was miraculously sent by divine command and conducted by the angel of the Lord to the King." Word of Joan's fabulous story of how she reached the Dauphin had travelled fast. Christine also knew of Joan's examination by theologians at Poitiers, but she made it clear that approval by mortals was not what made Joan believable; her authenticity is certified by the prophecies of Merlin, the Sibyl and Bede, who more than five hundred years before foresaw and wrote down all that Joan had done.

Christine glories that a woman has led the army to victory, boasting that "never did anyone see greater strength, even in hundreds or thousands of men!" But Christine also praises Joan in traditional feminine terms, claiming that she not only "casts the rebels down" but "feeds France with the sweet, nourishing milk of peace." Here we encounter Joan the androgyne, the little maid who smites Goliath, "a *woman* –a simple shepherdess–braver than any man

---

89. Thomassin is quoted in the Introduction to the *Ditié*, p. 5.

ever was in Rome." Christine's poem is but the first of many literary attempts to encompass in one image of Joan both the masculine, invincible warrior and the diminutive but potent young maid. The attempt fails, as it always must, given the limits of our concepts of masculine and feminine, but Christine's Joan does not slip into childishness, cloying innocence, nor passivity as do many later literary portraits of the Maid. Her Joan is an exciting heroine, more than a match for any man, on the battlefield or in mythology.

This glimpse of Joan, less than three months after she stepped into history at Orléans, goes far toward documenting how she could have seen herself as a magical leader. Her contemporaries accepted her as such: not only common people but, in this case, a sophisticated woman who had lived her life in court circles. Rich and poor alike were prepared to accept one divinely chosen, miraculously led person as the answer to France's crisis.

***

By the time that Christine de Pisan wrote her encomium, Joan had already fulfilled the main requirements to be a shaman. Called by her voices as she entered puberty, she experienced their presence for several years primarily in the out-of-doors, especially in settings long known as sacred or magical. Often summoned by the ringing of bells, the voices were accompanied by a mysterious light and always appeared spontaneously; she could not will their appearance. Acknowledging their power over her, Joan vowed to remain a virgin for as long as was necessary and, renouncing her ordinary condition, she became their instrument. She separated herself from her community, breaking off her romance and shunning dancing in order to partake of this intense spiritual experience. Having been pursued and educated by her voices for about five years, at a time of great crisis, both public (the burning of her village and the siege of Orléans) and private (her father's nightmare and threats against her) she finally took action on their counsel.

We have seen that no matter how fabulous an adept's ecstatic experiences may be, she does not become a shaman until she has first gained secret information and special powers *needed by her community* and, what is of ultimate importance, until she convinces her audience that hers is an authentic call. In the early winter of 1429 at Vaucouleurs, Joan began to win adherents, whereupon she adopted male clothing, cut her hair, named herself "Jehanne La Pucelle," and took up a soldier's life. In the following months at

Chinon she convinced the most powerful persons in France that she was of the spiritually elect, that she had access to a region of the sacred. By prophesying, proving her clairvoyance, and, what was most compelling, by leading the army to a series of victories, she won their confidence. It was confidence not in Joan's military or diplomatic skills, for she had few, but rather in Joan as a medium, as an authentic conduit for guidance from the spirit-world, from God. She brought her contemporaries swift release from their fear of destruction.

As Eliade has defined it, "seeing spirits, in dream or awake, is the determining sign of the shamanic vocation....Seeing them face to face, [the shaman] talks with them, prays to them, implores them."[90] Once Joan reached the Dauphin she spoke openly of her mystical experiences, claiming her prophecies and revelations as proof of her calling, and was accepted as the shaman sent to the French in their crisis. That this charismatic figure turned out to be a young girl was greeted with different responses, as we shall see. But for many French people in that catastrophic decade, a female saviour was a possibility.

Joan of Arc is one of those mortals seized by God, "above all else a God-inspired, God-intoxicated individualist."[91] Her life is an example of the times when the spirits break through ecclesiastical structures to possess, empower, and consume a Chosen One. Moving into the ready-made role of female prophet and magic worker, Joan seized with both hands the possibilities in her time and place to be a shamanistic leader. That the role required finally that she be consumed, that the shaman became the sacrificial hero was not revealed to her at the start. Joan did not choose to be a martyr; on the contrary, she tried to avoid that destiny with all her might. The personal vision that reaches us through Joan's words and actions is that of service, of accomplishing a mission. The martyrdom tells us more about the politics and religion of the ruling class than it does about Joan. Having investigated that inner fire which illumined her consciousness and guided her life, we must now turn to the account of how her human enemies consumed her.

90. Eliade, *Shamanism*, pp. 84, 88.
91. W.S. Scott, *Jeanne d'Arc*, p. 143.

Chapter Four
The Inquisition and the Individual:
Joan as Heretic

The Voice comes to me from God; and I do not tell you all I know about it; I have far greater fear of doing wrong in saying to you things that would displease it, than I have in answering you.
Joan, the Trial, February 24, 1431

On all that I am asked I will refer to the Church Militant, provided they do not command anything impossible. And I hold as a thing impossible to declare that my actions and my words...I have not done and said by the order of God: And in case the Church should wish me to do anything contrary to the command which has been given me of God, I will not consent to it, whatever it may be.

The Trial, March 31, 1431

Joan of Arc was condemned not as an enemy military leader but as a witch and a heretic. After Joan's capture in May, 1430, the theological faculty of the University of Paris moved immediately that she be put on trial for heresy in an ecclesiastical court. In a military era in which wars were financed out of ransom money, in which the capture of important enemies for ransom was a major strategic consideration, Joan was not put up for ransom, nor did the French king ever offer to buy her freedom. After her capture it was a foregone conclusion that the English wanted Joan dead, and Charles appears not to have cared what happened to her or even, perhaps, to have wanted to be rid of her.

The theologians had their way; the trial, lasting over three months, very long for a medieval case, was held in ecclesiastical court in Rouen. The condemnation record lists seventy accusations together with Joan's defenses against each of them;[1] but this was

1. Barrett, pp. 148-239. The material on the trial summation in Murray is incomplete.

only the first step in the summation. The seventy charges were then condensed into twelve articles, from which Joan's replies were all omitted. This summary and the court's conclusions were now sent to the theological faculty at the University of Paris, who accepted them, re-worded them, and forwarded them with comments to the new pope, Eugenius IV, and the cardinals.[2] The University's version was noticeably more libellous than the court's and indicted Joan more forcefully as a witch; the language, referring as it does to "evil opinions," "superstition," "divination," "idolatry," "blasphemy," "diabolical spirits," described Joan as totally demonic; and the version sent to the pope concluded that she was "an apostate...a liar and a witch."[3]

Because these indictments do not relate to military crimes, but come rather from the theology of diabolism, they warrant close scrutiny. The charges against her fell mainly into three categories. That she had used magic: by seeing, hearing, touching, smelling, and talking to her saints *as bodily creatures;* that she had seen and heard them at the fairies' tree, "an unhallowed spot;" that she claimed to know their identity, calling them St. Michael, St. Catherine, and St. Margaret, when in reality they were "Belial, Satan, and Behemoth;" that St. Michael made a bodily appearance to her king and gave him a magical sign of her mission, a shining crown; that she used sacred words and spells on her banner and ring and in her letters, in order to further a blasphemous mission; that she had caused herself to be adored and venerated, which was self-deification; that she had attempted to heal a dying baby; that her saints revealed many secrets to her—how to recognize Captain de Baudricourt and her king, where to find a sword at Fierbois, that she would be delivered from prison, that the French would win their greatest victories when she led them; and that when she attempted escape by jumping from a tower, she was magically unharmed. All of these things Joan had in fact claimed or in some form had done, except the claim about deification, but the tenor of the charges, linking her with spirits, cast them in a pernicious light. Because the demonic implications of these charges will be discussed in the next chapter, I will note here only that the accusations linking Joan with the devil, which make up more than half of her trial, were seen as doubly dangerous because they corrupted the common folk, who were supposed to have been led into idolatry by her fabulous claims.

2. Ibid., pp. 243-251 for the Rouen courts' summary of twelve articles; pp. 315-323 for the University of Paris version.

3. Barrett, pp. 315-317, 320.

The second group of accusations charged that she went against the church's norms for a lay person, and especially for a woman. The judges saw Joan as headstrong and arrogant, faults of which she was indeed guilty. They reminded her that she had rashly insisted on attacking Paris on a feast day of the Virgin Mary, and had ordered an enemy captain killed (not offered for ransom), which was against the customs of warfare. Most of the charges of pride, however, centered on Joan's audacity to act even though she was female. Had she not gone to Vaucouleurs to join the army without her parents' knowledge and against their express command? Had she not lived among men, without women companions, leading the life of a soldier? Her judges inflated her insistence that the saints were entirely on the French side into charges that she wantonly murdered the enemy and shed blood without remorse. And the accusation of cutting her hair and wearing men's clothes, especially of receiving communion in male attire, taking up as it did so many pages of the trial record, indicates how grievously shocked the judges were by her transvestism.

The final set of charges received far less space but carried an even more ominous indictment than those of sorcery and pride. From Joan's not reporting her magical messages to a priest, to her claim that she would go to Paradise, the judges bore down hardest on her refusal to accept the authority and the judgments of the church. They objected that she claimed to be sent by God, that she consecrated her virginity to her saints, that she accepted absolution (for jumping from the tower) from her saints, that she was certain that she was not in mortal sin, and that by every measure she had placed her visions in the position of final authority over her, where the judgments of the church should be. They summed up their condemnation of her in the final article, averring that "she does not submit herself to the judgment of the Church Militant, or to that of living men, but to God alone," whom, they said, she claimed to know through her diabolical voices.

To the modern student of Joan's life it is clear that much of what went on at the trial was not in response to Joan's testimony (most of which was corroborated at the retrial some thirty years later) but expressed the concerns, fears, and beliefs of her judges. In order to understand their judgment of Joan, we must look at two prominent features of fifteenth-century religion: the fear of heresy and the institution which the church had created in the 1230s to combat that fear, the inquisition.

What was heresy? From the start, it had been defined as one's

pursuit of what to the individual seemed right.[4] While that may
sound innocuous enough to us today, praise-worthy even, by a
church that was fast losing its dominance in European culture it was
seen as treason, as an offense to both God and society.

Jeffrey Russell's definition, that heresy is whatever the pope
decrees to be heretical, is accurate enough, and leads us to the useful
conclusion of Herbert Grundmann, that it was the clergy who largely
determined whether a lay person or lay movement would *become*
heretical or would find a useful, orthodox role in the church–
whether, in short, a lay person would become a heretic or a saint. "If
the clergy had not 'hereticated' the Waldensians, for instance, they
might not in fact have become heretical."[5] That is, when the clergy
applied hostile pressure to a person or a group, they forced them to
become more radical; the church itself, therefore, created heresy.

Joan's trial is a case in point: she appears never to have thought–
never to have had to think–whether her voices were an authority
higher than the church, until her inquisitors put the question to her:

Will you refer yourself to the decision of the Church?

I refer myself to God who sent me, to Our Lady, and to all the
Saints in Paradise. And in my opinion it is all one, God and the
Church; and one should make no difficulty about it. Why do you
make a difficulty?

Thus spiritualizing the church, Joan put herself in dangerous waters;
but she was not aware of her danger. Only when the judge insisted
that in the matter of her obedience to the church he meant the
Church Militant, the visible church, human and yet incapable of
erring–only then did Joan realize that she must choose:

I came to the King of France from God...and the Church
Victorious above, and by their command. To this Church I submit
all my good deeds....As to saying whether I will submit myself to
the Church Militant, I will not now answer anything more.[6]

4. Walter L. Wakefield and Austin P. Evans, eds., *Heresies of the High Middle Ages*
(New York: Columbia University Press, 1969), p. 2.

5. Jeffrey Russell, *Dissent and Reform in the Early Middle Ages* (Berkeley: University
of California Press, 1965), p. 5; Grundmann's thesis in *Religiöse Bewegungen im
Mittelalter* is summarized by Richard Kieckhefer in "Radical Tendencies in the
Flagellant Movement of the Mid-Fourteenth Century," *Journal of Medieval and
Renaissance Studies*, 4 (1977):157-176; see pp. 173-174.

6. Murray, pp. 86-87.

The church in the early middle ages had declared simply that orthodoxy meant accepting the defined body of faith; it had left so many matters undefined that a free-thinking Christian might wander far and not be noticed. It was because of loosely-defined doctrine that folk and elite religions were able to coexist for so long. By Joan's time, that had changed. Canonists and scholastics were far along with the task of defining the Christian faith more narrowly, leaving few loopholes for the rebellious, the foolhardy, or the naive. Since Joan gave no hint of being drawn to reformist rebellion, and was certainly no fool, we have to assume that she fell unsuspecting into a trap not yet clearly labelled by her church, to find herself charged with spiritual arrogance. Joan saw herself as a chosen leader; her judges interpreted that as pride blasphemous and demonic.

The more the late medieval church encountered dissent, the more rigid became its defenses against it. Although England was a country not much troubled by dissent, the year 1428 had seen a number of actions taken against heretics there. In the year before Joan began her mission, an apparent recurrence of Lollard belief in eastern England had led to the arrest of sixty suspects, three of whom were burned to death by the Bishop of Norwich, who later became an observer at Joan's trial. The remains of John Wyclif (spiritual founder of the Lollards) were dug up and burned. And in English-held lands in France in the same year as Joan's condemnation, heresy trials were held at Tournai, Mons, and Valenciennes; twenty suspects were summoned at Lille, of whom at least eight were burned.[7]

In the eyes of the ruling class, one must remember, ecclesiastical revolt was combined with economic and political upheaval. In 1381 England had been shaken by a Peasants' Revolt, an attempted revolution demanding congregational control of churches along with land reform. Although the peasants were ruthlessly put down, a remnant of dissent lingered on in the Lollards, who were labelled "communists" whether they believed in sharing wealth or not.

There are scant parallels between Joan's simple, devout beliefs and the fierce anti-sacramentalism and anti-clericalism of the Lollards, but on two important counts she was enough like them to alarm the English and French theologians. Lollards refused to take oaths (Joan resisted taking the oath every time she was asked) and were anti-authoritarian. That is, they rebelled against the need for a

7. Malcolm Vale, "Jeanne d'Arc, victime d'une guerre civile?", *Colloque d'histoire médiévale*, Orléans, Octobre 1979 (Centre national de la recherche scientifique), pp. 207, 211. My thanks to Prof. Vale for making this paper available to me.

licensed cleric to preach and for a priest to hear confession, insisting that the members of their sect could perform these functions, and Joan had declared her own spiritual independence from the priesthood.

A much larger and more threatening group, the Hussites in Bohemia, had moved into full, armed rebellion against the pope, whose stern demand to the English for a crusading army to crush them was put aside when, irony of ironies, the English diverted that army to France to be used against Joan's soldiers. That the English could get away with ordering troops vowed to extirpate heresy, who enjoyed thereby full absolution for any killing they might commit, to fight against the pope's French subjects shows the extent to which Joan and her army were perceived as troops of the Devil.[8] It also indicates the extent to which Joan was seen as interchangeable with the followers of Hus, with their cry for an autonomous religion. On that issue, Joan's insistence that her saints offered her not only guidance but absolution *and the assurance of salvation* made her look suspiciously like the heretical sects.

We have seen how easily mysticism, hard to supervise, impossible to destroy, became heresy in the eyes of the church. As Malcolm Vale observed, "Like other mystics and visionaries, [Joan] posed a threat to the hierarchy of the Church. If men were able to communicate so directly with God–through visions or 'voices'–what need was there for the clergy?" Vale concluded that, on this basis, Joan "was no friend of the earthly Church Militant."[9]

In addition to making the services of the church redundant, Joan's absolute faith in her visions carried the added punch of making her appear larger than life to her contemporaries. Immediately after her first victory at Orléans, English troops began to exhibit an hysterical fear of her. A levy of English reinforcements refused to embark for France because they believed that her power, being demonic, was invincible. The English regent, the Duke of Bedford, writing to the young Henry VI three years after Joan's death, still evoked her memory with horror, feeling still the need to explain her power as supernatural. To condone the English defeat at Orléans he claimed that the French:

---

8. John A.F. Thomson, *The Later Lollards, 1414-1520* (Oxford University Press, 1965), p. 241ff. George Holmes, "Cardinal Beaufort and the Crusade against the Hussites," *EHR* 42 (October 1973):721-750.

9. Vale, *Charles VII*, p. 47.

hadde of a disciple and leme of the feende called the Pucelle that used fake enchantements and sorcerie, the which stroke and discomfiture not only lessed in greet partie the nombre of youre peuple ther, but aswel withdrewe the courage of the remenaunt in marvaillous wise....[10]

In identifying Joan with the Devil, the English leaders, as well as the Parisian theologians, were placing her in that "other religion," that religion of the people which they more and more feared. As Malcolm Vale reminds us, it was the common people and the ordinary soldiers who continued to believe in Joan.[11] The aristocracy whom she took such pleasure in moving among deserted her and lost faith in her as soon as she stopped winning battles. The simple people, who believed in the kind of visions, signs, and prophecies that Joan excelled in, continuously looked for magic-working women, and when they found one as successful and appealing as Joan, they believed in her, even, if necessary, against the commands of the clergy. In a word, they believed in Joan's authority–her voices–above the teachings of the church. Thus it was not only Joan who was out of control. Her pernicious influence was spreading in France, and had not the Lollard movement in England and, even more, the Hussite rebellion in Bohemia, shown the fifteenth-century ruling class what could happen? Although Joan cannot be credited with a single belief smacking of political or economic revolution, and although she inspired no actual movement in the religious sphere, still one must acknowledge that, given the unstable state of late medieval society, the ruling class had reason to fear her.

10. Vale, "Jeanne d'Arc....," p. 205, quoted from the *Proceedings and Ordinances of the Privy Council of England, 1386-1542*, 4:223. The reference to English troops was made by Champion, in Barrett, p. 510.

11. Vale, "Jeanne d'Arc...," p. 209: "Après tout, c'était le peuple et les simples soldats qui croyaient en Jeanne. Si ces 'simples' tenaient plus compte des femmes qui s'attribuaient une autorité sacrée que des doctrines de l'Eglise, telles que le clergé les enseignait, on pouvait craindre de voir périr la vraie religion et l'Eglise tomber dans le puits sans fond de Satan. Au delà des charges soutenues contre Jeanne, en 1431, on percevait, dans le clergé et dans les classes dirigeantes une crainte, exagérée mais profonde, de l'hétérodoxie."

Deborah Fraioli raises the somewhat different possibility that even among the noble class, heterodox ideas existed: "Much of what Joan of Arc proclaimed agreed with a number of unorthodox medieval religious views which despite their irregularity appear to have been cherished by many of Joan's contemporaries. To the delight of everyone, Joan of Arc seemed to confirm that God would still intervene directly in human affairs...." "The Literary Image of Joan of Arc," p. 829.

Vale's conclusion is worth pondering:

> Fundamentally, Joan of Arc is neither the victim of English polit-
> ical vengeance nor of civil war among the French. One must
> rather see her condemnation in the light of the generalized fear
> of heresy which gripped all those who governed, secular and
> ecclesiastical. The nobles, even her early admirers, never felt
> entirely sure about the source of her power, and the theologians
> were certain that such a deviant person must be heterodox.
> Therefore there was no place, in the mind and the sympathies of
> her examiners, for warriors who had visions and heard voices.[12]

***

Two days after Joan was taken prisoner, the theological faculty at
the University of Paris wrote her Burgundian captors to insist that
Joan be turned over to the inquisitor of France to be tried as a
heretic; this faculty, long under the control of the English, had
produced a political theory justifying the incorporation of France
with England under one monarch–the English king. Opposed to Joan
therefore on political grounds, the theological faculty had double
reason to want her in its grasp, for it had long considered itself the
pope's chief arbiter of orthodoxy and, hence, the intellectual scourge
of deviancy in the church. Not only holding "itself to be the real
head of Christendom," it also "held itself to be the real head of the
Kingdom of France;" given its English loyalties, it was the mortal
enemy of Charles VII.

The English, meanwhile, were not idle, having appointed a former
rector of the University, Bishop Pierre Cauchon, to negotiate the
purchase of Joan from the Burgundians for the same purpose–to try
her for heresy. Having been driven out of his bishopric at Beauvais
by Charles VII's army, resurgent under Joan's inspiration, Cauchon
had personal reasons for revenge in addition to the fact of his
having been in the pay of the English since at least 1419.[13] He
finally managed to buy Joan from the Burgundians for 6,000 francs,
plus a pension to her captor.

---

12. Vale, "Jeanne d'Arc...," p. 216, my translation.
13. The quotation about the University of Paris is from Pernoud, *Joan of Arc*, p.
238; the information about Cauchon is from Pernoud, pp. 130, 156-157, and from
Marot, *Joan the Good Lorrainer*, pp. 21-22.

For about four months Joan remained in Burgundian prisons at Belvoir and Beaurevoir. When she learned that she was to be handed over to the English, she knew that was her death warrant, and she panicked. Preferring immediate death to captivity and death at English hands, she managed to slip out a window of the tower of Beaurevoir. Although her voices commanded her not to take her own life, she reported that "...I could not control myself; when my Voices saw my need...they saved my life and kept me from killing myself."[14] This was not exactly the miraculous deliverance Joan may have hoped for from St. Catherine, that promoter of prison breaks, but after all, her saints had repeatedly warned her not to try to escape.

The English brought her to Rouen and held her in a military prison where she was guarded by English jailers. Joan had the worst of two worlds: an *ecclesiastical* court charging her with heresy, for which the penalty was death by fire, rather than a military tribunal offering a less fearsome execution; and a *military* prison, where she was denied female attendants and risked humiliation and attempted rape by the men who guarded her.

The trial was soon set up, Bishop Cauchon co-presiding with the vice-inquisitor of France, and over one hundred theologians commissioned to hear the charges, of whom thirty or forty were usually present at the public sessions. Of the one-hundred-three men involved, all but eight were French. And yet, while the charges were drawn up, the prosecution carried out, and the verdict handed down by Frenchmen, it was the English who master-minded the proceedings. They paid the bills. Their money lured many of the theologians who attended from Paris and from the cathedral chapters at Rouen and Beauvais. Whenever the least suspicion of leniency leaked out from the court, the English generals were quick to complain.

In the past, some French historians and iconographers have tried to place the burden of guilt for Joan's condemnation onto the English.[15] It was a futile exercise, for the trial record makes clear the total complicity of both parties, with not a clean hand among them. One or two voices were raised to question the proceedings: a cleric who observed on the second day that "it was dangerous to start that trial" was summarily thrown into jail; and another, after showing partiality to Joan, was said (although this proved incorrect) to have had to flee Rouen. The truth is that among a hundred

14. Murray, pp. 74-75, 83.
15. See, for example, Lionel Royer's wall paintings in the nave of the basilica dedicted to Joan outside Domremy, installed in 1909, as described below.

learned, well-to-do clerics, scarcely a one gave any hint of believing Joan. One lone voice was raised, from the safe distance of the retrial proceedings twenty-one years after the process at Rouen. A priest named Jean Lefevre had tried to protest that a theological question put to Joan "was not a suitable question for such a girl," but Cauchon had silenced him. Now, in hindsight, he admitted that Joan had answered her inquisitors with such prudence that "for the space of three weeks I believed her to be inspired." But even this sympathetic witness hedged, allowing that his admiration for her performance covered everything "with the exception of the subject of her revelations from God."[16]

That the judges feared her we may be sure—she was a proven prophetess and seer, and a shamanic war leader of awesome reputation. But her judges did not evidence rational doubt or critical questioning about the case. For all their training as canonists, philosophers, diplomats, they eschewed analysis, moving straight toward a law-and-order decision. The verdict, to no one's surprise, was unanimous.

Another kind of guilt-shifting still goes on, this time on the part of the church. When the campaign for Joan's canonization was in full swing during the first decades of this century, the French church attempted to erase its guilt in the trial proceedings by its choice of iconography for the new basilica built in Joan's honor just outside Domremy: the eight huge wall paintings which dominate the nave, showing the heroine's life, faithfully record each major event—first appearance of the voices, the coronation of Charles at Rheims, and so on,—but omit the trial. Joan's death, duly represented in a moving portrayal of the young heroine at the stake, is explained by the vulgar, blood-thirsty faces of the English soldiers. The French clergy are shown trying to relieve her dying agonies, but the trial, that three-month-long climactic ordeal carried out by the French church, appears not to have happened.[17]

Church historians have tried several ways of getting around the French church's duplicity in Joan's death. George Tavard claims that the trial was not authentic, having been manipulated by the English to the point of fraud; in fact, Cauchon scrupulously followed the rules for an inquisitional court. John A. O'Brien, while critical of

16. Pierre Champion, "On the Trial of Jeanne d'Arc," in Barrett, p. 508. Lefevre's testimony is in Murray, p. 210.

17. In an inspection of the Johannic iconography in half a dozen churches in the region of Domremy, including the cathedral at Toul, I found only one reference to the trial, a stained glass window dedicated to that theme in the parish church at Domremy.

both French and English motives and sympathetic to Joan, never mentions the issue which Joan defended to her death: her rejection of the authority of the church. In this he follows the canonization proceedings, which managed to declare Joan a saint while ignoring the principal reason for which she had been condemned as a heretic.[18]

As for the defendant, not out of her teens, in chains, illiterate, the only female among several hundred male guards and jurors, Joan managed to create a brilliant, if unsuccessful, defense. Day after day she fielded trick questions, the same ones put to her over and over in differing form, questions based on intricate theological knowledge, and what was harder, questions based on her judges' gross belief in demonic witchcraft. The questions pushed her relentlessly into the witch-hunters' trap, playing on the established doctrine about demons, that their bodies are corporeal, whereas the saints' are ethereal.

Did you see Saint Michael and these Angels bodily and in reality?

How do you know whether the object that appears to you is male or female?

These saints who show themselves to you, do they have any hair?...Is there anything between their crowns and hair? [Meaning horns.]

Joan: No.

Does not St. Margaret speak English?

Joan: Why should she speak English when she is not on the English side?

18. On the trial: George Tavard, *Woman in Christian Tradition* (South Bend: University of Notre Dame Press, 1973), p. 217; John A. O'Brien, *The Inquisition* (New York: Macmillan, 1973), p. 155ff. On the canonization: William Searle, *The Saint and the Skeptics: Joan of Arc in the Works of Mark Twain, Anatole France, and Bernard Shaw* (Detroit: Wayne State University Press, 1976), pp. 139-144. The brief papal pronouncement at the canonization is printed in *Joan of Arc: Fact, Legend, and Literature,* eds. Wilfred T. Jewkes and Jerome B. Landfield (New York: Harcourt, Brace, and World, 1964), pp. 165-166. In the Roman calendar of saints, Joan is listed merely as "Virgin," not as "Martyr."

Even harder to take were questions based on the belief that demons used their bodies to seduce women into the service of the devil:

In what likeness did Saint Michael appear to you?...Was he naked?

Joan: Do you think God has not wherewithal to clothe him?

Had he hair?

Joan: Why should it have been cut off?...

If the devil were to put himself in the form or likeness of an angel, how would you know if it were a good or an evil angel?

Joan: I should know quite well if it were Saint Michael or a counterfeit....

What part of Saint Catherine did you touch?

Joan: You will have no more about it from me!

Did you ever kiss or embrace Saint Catherine or Saint Margaret?

Joan: I have embraced them both.

Did they smell good?

Joan: It is well to know that they smelled good.

In embracing them, did you feel any heat or anything else?

Joan: I could not have embraced them without feeling and touching them.

What part did you kiss—face or feet?

Joan: It is more proper and respectful to kiss their feet.

Having established to their satisfaction that Joan had trafficked with the devil, her inquisitors were now ready to spring the question that would trap her into heresy.

Do you know if you are in the Grace of God? Joan's reply was astonishingly clever, wise, and moving:

> If I am not, may God place me there; if I am, may God keep
> me....But if I were in a state of sin, do you think the Voice would
> come to me?[19]

Worse than the offensive implications of the questions was the
very structure of the trial. The procedure of the inquisition was radi-
cally different from that of traditional church courts. In 1231, in
order to grapple with what it deemed an enormous threat, the
church had established the papal inquisition, a category of tribunals
for which it gradually built up a special set of rules, and these were
what confronted and confounded Joan. The accused was required to
take an oath which would require her to testify against herself. Each
time Joan was asked to swear the court's oath she objected, because
she could not reveal secrets told her by her voices. The accused was
denied all counsel. Although Joan had asked for counsel early in the
trial, she was denied, and stood against her judges absolutely alone;
she had no lawyers or legal experts to help guide her through the
maze of questioning. Not even her family could see her, although
her two younger brothers were in Rouen at the time of the trial, one
of them having been captured with her.

There was no appeal from inquisitional courts, not even to the
Apostolic See; late in her trial Joan asked to appeal to the pope but
was denied. Refusal to answer questions led to imprisonment, but
this was a hollow threat to Joan, already in solitary confinement. She
put off difficult questions as long as she dared, but as her day of
sentencing approached, she tried to satisfy the judges on every point,
even on the matter of her special sign to the king.[20]

It was legal for inquisitors to plant spies to collect disclosures of
guilt. One of the priests who visited Joan's cell, ostensibly to talk her
into confessing, was actually a spy. Next to her cell there was a small
hidden room from which she was observed. It was legal also to use
torture to compel a recalcitrant prisoner to confess; Joan was threatened with torture, but the sanction was not carried out. All the
property of the condemned person was to be confiscated, half of it
usually going to the court, whether ecclesiastical or, as was the case
increasingly after Joan's time, secular, and half to the accusers. As

19. Murray, pp. 25, 39-40, 42, 84, 92. As questions like these were repeated day
after day, the slant moved toward the more explicit, the more physical.

20. The material on procedures of the inquisition is taken from O'Brien, *The
Inquisition*, pp. 12-25. For my comments on Richard Kieckhefer's views, see above,
chap. 2, n. 36.

Joan had neither property nor other wealth, greed cannot have been a motive in her case.

By the fifteenth century, inquisitional courts had a long, successful history in wiping out heresy, and were being used increasingly to ferret out the church's new enemies, the witches. Both types of charges were terribly damaging against Joan, but it was indictment of spiritual independence which destroyed her. In the summation of the charges, the ultimate accusation was that Joan had taken on the authority of God and raised herself above the power of the church by neither confessing her visions to a priest nor asking any cleric for guidance in or approval of her supernatural experiences. The argument is telling:

> Joan: First, as to that on which you admonish me for my good and for our Faith, I thank you and all the company also; as to the advice which you offer me, also I thank you; but I have no intention of desisting from the counsel of Our Lord....
>
> Will you refer yourself to the judgment of the Church on earth for all you have said or done, be it good or bad?...
>
> Joan: ...in case the Church should wish me to do anything contrary to the command which has been given me of God, I will not consent to it, whatever it may be.
>
> If the Church Militant tells you that your revelations are illusions, or diabolical things, will you defer to the Church?
>
> Joan: I will defer to God, Whose Commandment I always do. I know well that that which is contained in my Case has come to me by the Commandment of God; what I affirm in the Case is, that I have acted by the order of God: it is impossible for me to say otherwise. In case the Church should prescribe the contrary, I should not refer to any one in the world, but to God alone, Whose Commandment I always follow.[21]

Here, I believe, Joan placed herself among those few who can be called autonomous–persons not guided by spiritual confessors nor protected by clerics in powerful positions, who place their faith entirely in their own religious experience. Given the struggle which the church was just completing against the Wyclifites and its contin-

21. Murray, pp. 102-104.

uing desperate attempt to repress the Hussites in Bohemia, Joan's affirmation of her voices–that is, of the truth of her independent revelations, or, of the primacy of her conscience over the beliefs maintained by her inquisitors–was bound to damn her as a heretic. I have no evidence that Joan knew the teachings of Wyclif (she may have heard of Hus) and I am convinced that Joan did not seek to change or to reform the church in any way. And yet, under the threat of death she still maintained that she knew the truth, independent of the church's channels of authority. In that belief, she shared with Lollard and Hussite a radical commitment to follow what the individual knows to be right.

Joan declared herself to be a messenger from God, a fit channel for God's word to enter this world. Where did she get such ideas? Her affirmation of her belief in the validity of her own religious experience was unshakable. As W.S. Scott wrote,

> ...in the person of the Maid the ecclesiastical world of her day saw (and saw clearly for the first time) a new figure, of whom they were rightly afraid–the figure of one who throughout her short life claimed the absolute validity of her own religious experience...above all else a God-inspired, God-intoxicated individualist.[22]

She defied the powers of her church and of an enemy nation on this point: that she was an authentic conduit from the spirit world, from the "King of Heaven," to her people and her king in this world. In words that would do proud Gerrard Winstanley or Anne Hutchinson, Joan expressed her determination "not to desist from the counsel of the Lord," no matter what the church visible said or did to her.

Where did Joan find these words? She had no reformist congregation to support her in her stand. The most cruel fact of her horrifying end was that there was not one human being around her who understood what the nature of her mission had been. But in her society there had been, and still were, the mystics, the women who put their own counsel above the teachings of the church. From the tradition established by unknowns and folk heroes alike, from the witness of Prous Boneta, Constance de **Rabastens**, Marie Robine, Pierrone, came the model, the very possibility, to experience what Joan had lived through and then to defend it with integrity.

22. W.S. Scott, *Jeanne d'Arc* (London, 1974), p. 140.

***

The standard penalty for heretical conviction was death at the stake, and the same sentence applied to witchcraft, which was by Joan's time seen as a form of heresy (i.e., witches believed in the Devil). We know that Joan had assumed that she would meet a more humane execution than burning, for she had asked to be buried in consecrated ground. When informed on the morning of her execution that she was to be burned, she was reported to tear her hair and cry out, "Alas, am I to be so horribly and cruelly treated? Alas! that my body, whole and entire, which has never been corrupted, should today be consumed and burned to ashes!"[23]

Joan was indeed an authentic heroine, a destiny which she had avidly courted. But she had never wanted to be a martyr. None of Joan's language, direct and commonsensical as it was, indicates that she courted suffering or death. We see that she made a sacrificial death; she knew only that she died forsaken, in ignominy and in the most terrible pain, excommunicated, condemned to hell, having had no word from her allies in over a year of captivity.

Neither had she ever wanted to be a heretic. For all Joan's pride and incredible belief in herself, she had truly loved the church. And yet she was indeed a heretic, and the church had reason to condemn her. That is, she witnessed to a power antithetical to the medieval church. Ultimately, she stood for that ancient but ever-growing strand in European religion, the religion of the spirit, the experience of the mystic, or as we would say, the voice of conscience, the individual, inner voice. The church attempted to control this through its doctrine of sin: "the medieval Christian was [seen as] always sinning, always beginning anew, always returning to the sacraments for short-lived strength and assurance."[24] The theologians at Paris could not have put it better than in their deliberations on the Twelve Articles charged against Joan: "This woman sins when she says she is as certain of being received into Paradise as if she were already a partaker of that blessed glory, seeing that on this earthly journey no pilgrim knows if he is worthy of glory or of punishment, which the sovereign judge alone can tell."[25]

At Joan's trial, two forms of European medieval Christianity clashed. One was the official religion of the nobility and the educated, the latter being mostly higher clergy and theologians. The

---

23. Murray, p. 158, testimony of Br. Jean Toutmouillé at the retrial.
24. Ozment, *The Age of Reform*, pp. 30-31.
25. Barrett, pp. 320-321.

other was the popular religion of the countryside. It included many ideas and practices which were older than the church. For centuries the official church had called these practices pagan and had uneasily coexisted with them. Upgrading paganism now by identifying it with the "ancient fiend," the church of the fifteenth century increasingly labelled it witchcraft, created an elaborate mythology/theology about it, and in effect promoted it to the rank of a full, rival religion which the church hierarchy determined to destroy. It was Joan's fate to be crushed in this turn of history.

A generation earlier Joan, like Marie Robine, might have lived out her life as an honored prophetess, supported by the church. To be sure, the church had begun before that to fear and punish female seers: in 1310 Marguerite Porete was one of the first to be condemned. But Joan, growing up in Domremy in the 1420s, watching her country being devoured by war, had good reason to believe that when she offered to save France she would be listened to. She came late in the day, but she was a true folk hero, a genuine shamanic inspirée. It was her cruel fate to bring her authentic gifts of leadership and prophecy to a time and place in which they would trigger a profound fear.

Prohetic vision, miraculous success in battle, fanatic belief in her own channels of grace–all in a virginal woman. In the eyes of the ecclesiastical hierarchy and nobility, these added up to a power too deviant and too strong. They called this power witchcraft.

Chapter Five
Women, the Devil, and Sexuality:
Joan as Witch

...the said woman is blasphemous towards God, contemptuous of God in His sacraments, unmindful of divine and sacred law...foolishly boastful, and must be suspected of idolatry...she has imitated the rites of the heathen...[she is] a caller up of evil spirits, a wanderer from the faith...a liar and witch when she says she is sent from God....
Faculty of Theology, University of Paris
May, 1431

***

Not satisfied by including a heresy charge among Joan's alleged crimes, her enemies added the accusation that she was a witch. As one of the earliest processes using witchcraft charges against a major political figure, Joan's trial stands at the beginning of a particularly lurid period in European juridical history, when witch accusations, now clearly identified as heresy, grew apace and fear of witches increased, especially among the ruling class. As secular and ecclesiastical rulers grew more fearful of social unrest, they found deviance where before none had been.

Institutional religion reacted to the challenge of its late medieval problems in two ways: by increasingly appropriating the practices of magic to its own priesthood, and by declaring those who had authority in local religion to be witches. The local magicians were turned into figures, first of evil, later of derision. In studying this process in northern France and Flanders, Muchembled concludes that the increasing frequency of "witch trials was one sign of the long battle to break down popular culture," a victory at long last of the Roman priesthood over local seers.[1]

---

1. Robert Muchembled, "The Witches of the Cambrésis," in *Religion and the People: 800-1700*, p. 268.

Joan lived in a time of increasing official concern over witchcraft, when the long-standing uses of magic on which rural Europe had depended were for the first time violently attacked by the church.[2] Having looked upon magic as sorcery, as the relatively harmless practice of individuals in rural areas, the ruling classes of Europe now began to believe in it themselves and to see it as diabolism, as the work of the Devil. In the process, some theologians promoted Satan to the role of arch-rival of Christ; his demons became worthy adversaries of the saints and angels, and a vast new web of mythology/theology was spun. Eventually, the priesthood converted the villagers to their view of the matter: ordinary magic became devil worship; an effective part of folk culture became heresy. But this process required the two centuries following Joan's death to become effective.

As long as they were in competition with the local magic-workers, however, the Christian priesthood had to prove whose magic produced the true miracle. As medieval religion became more individualized, church officials began hauling the more powerful visionaries and healers into court under charges of sorcery and diabolism. Because the largest percentage of these spiritually gifted individuals were female, this purge created a persecution by gender.

In establishing the authority of its priesthood over female spiritual adepts, the church had two powerful fears to play upon: the society's traditional beliefs about women as highly sexed, irrational, and hard to control[3] and the general acknowledgment that human sexuality is also powerful, mysterious and never entirely under control. The church united these two already related fears by its ancient insistence that sexuality pertains more to females than males. Having asserted, moreover, from its beginning that women must be subordinate to and controlled by men, the church now contributed a mythology of witchcraft in which women were described as magically powerful, thereby producing a full-blown doctrine of the potential evil

2. A useful survey of this gradual growth of official condemnation against "witches" can be found in Jeffrey B. Russell, *Witchcraft in the Middle Ages* (Seacaucus: Citadel Press, 1972), chaps. 6-9; for my criticism of Russell's conclusion about Joan, see below, n. 5. Richard Kieckhefer made an important contribution toward tracing the change from belief in sorcery to diabolism in *European Witch Trials: Their Foundations in Popular and Learned Culture, 1300-1500* (Berkeley: University of California Press, 1976); one factor in this upgrading of sorcery was the charge that witchcraft was now heresy. Kieckhefer comments of the period just prior to Joan's mission that "the stereotypes earlier found in heresy trials now increasingly [were] transferred to witch trials" (p. 22).

3. Frances and Joseph Gies, *Women in the Middle Ages* (New York: Barnes and Noble, 1978), chap. 4.

inherent in women's nature.[4] That the great majority of witch trial victims were female is not surprising,[5] given that several of the church's teachings about women contributed to their conviction. Charges against women were often of a sexual nature, accusing them of bewitching men with love potions, rendering men impotent, causing their genitals to disappear, having sexual relations with the Devil or his demons, triggering abortions, or giving birth to demon babies. By combining charges of magical powers and of dangerous sexuality, the courts rendered the suspected witch a doubly threatening figure.[6]

Fears of folk magic, of its primary practitioners, women, and of the newly enhanced Devil figure coalesced into a vicious form of persecution. As the medieval period came to an end, societal fears which had been focused on heretics, Jews, and Muslims now were concentrated on an enemy in the midst of Christian society itself, the sorceress, newly seen as an agent of the Devil.

Secular rulers as well as ecclesiastics were becoming more fearful. Shaken by a century of peasant and urban uprisings, the nobility of Europe were trying to tighten the reins of control. It is not surprising, therefore, that this fear had infected the municipal authorities: there were precedents for secular persecution of witches in Paris as recently as 1390-1391. At two secular trials not involving the inquisition, four women were accused of sexual crimes (rendering a man impotent, bewitching another man into marriage, making him gravely ill) and were tortured into confessing bizarre relationships with bodily demons; all four were burned at the stake.[7]

4. Belief in the inherent evil of women and their subsequent identification as witches has been documented in a number of works, including Wolfgang Lederer, *The Fear of Women* (New York, 1968), Vern Bullough, *The Subordinate Sex: A History of Attitudes toward Women* (Urbana: University of Illinois Press, 1976), H.R. Hays, *The Dangerous Sex: The Myth of Feminine Evil* (New York: Pocket Books, 1964), esp. chaps. 14 and 15.

5. Russell, *Witchcraft in the Middle Ages*, pp. 279-285. Russell is incorrect in stating that the witchcraft charges against Joan of Arc were dropped. The summary of charges quoted at the beginning of this chapter, as well as the sermon of the Grand Inquisitor preached after her death (see my pp. 104-05) shows that the belief that Joan was a devil-inspired witch was not put aside.

6. The classic theological statement is found in Heinrich Kramer and James Sprenger, *Malleus Maleficarum* (Lyons, 1484), trans. Montague Summers (London, 1928; New York, 1971), a handbook for witchhunters published with papal approval and enormously influential in shaping the great witch craze of the sixteenth and seventeenth centuries. An important study of the persecutions is found in H.R. Trevor-Roper, *The European Witch-Craze* (New York: Harper Torchbooks, 1968). No historian of European witchcraft has yet taken full account of its gender issue, i.e. that the majority of the accused were women.

What is most interesting about these cases is that the final charges were not concerned with the above-mentioned maleficium but were based on blasphemy against the Trinity and the Gospels–in effect, theological charges. The secular courts, not only the theologians, were contributing to the new understanding of witchcraft as heresy.

While no witch persecution in the fifteenth century could compare with the awesome conflagrations that lay ahead, still people could begin to expect the occasional spectacular auto-da-fé. To take just one decade, in the ten years around the date of Joan's death, 1428-1438, approximately two hundred sixty persons were brought to trial in western Europe for some form of *sortilegium* and many were put to death.[8] The charges indicate that an hysterical imagination was developing in matters concerning the Devil: one man burned as an invoker of demons, another for causing storms, still another for sacrificing his baby daughter to the Devil; a priest tried for invocation of demons and necromancy; women burned, beheaded or drowned for killing children, practicing "love magic," inflicting illness.[9]

Out of this hodge-podge of traditional sorcery practices and new demonology, the most notorious case to emerge after Joan's was that of her comrade-in-arms and great admirer, Gilles de Rais, one of France's wealthiest nobles. A lover of children's beauty, Gilles may have found his homosexuality stirred by Joan's androgynous appearance as youthful Maid-in-armor.[10] Devoting himself to her, he fought beside her at Orléans, Patay, and Paris; he escorted the priest

7. Russell, *Witchcraft in the Middle Ages*, pp. 214-215. That secular rulers were also using witch accusations against political enemies is documented by two notorious French cases of the early fifteenth century: John, duke of Burgundy, had murdered the Armagnac Louis of Orléans in 1407, accusing him of invocation of demons, sorcery, witchcraft, necromancy, attempting to drive the king insane, to poison him, to set fire to his clothes, etc.; the Dauphin Charles or his henchmen had carried out the retaliatory murder of Duke John in 1419. After each of these assassinations the victim's hand was cut off, because it had been guided by sorcery and the invocation of demons: Vale, *Charles VII*, p. 29.

8. Although it is impossible to gain an exact count from the records, some of which refer only to "numerous persons," I culled this estimate from Kieckhefer's "calendar of Witch Trials," in *European Witch Trials*, pp. 122-125, which makes fascinating reading.

9. Ibid.; and Russell, *Witchcraft in the Middle Ages*, pp. 256-259.

10. Charles Williams, *Witchcraft* (New York: Meridian Books, 1949), pp. 116ff. Gilles' most recent biographer, Jean Benedetti, analyzes Gilles' attraction to Joan differently, stressing the Maid's asexual quality, seeing it as non-threatening to a man with sadistic sexual impulses: *Gilles de Rais* (New York: Stein and Day, 1972), pp. 188-189.

who carried the Holy Water at the Dauphin's coronation, and he raised money for Joan's forces. She is reported to have called on him for aid when she was wounded during the attack she led on Paris; beyond that we do not know what she thought of him. After her capture he returned to his ancestral estates and launched into a monstrous career of crime. In collaboration with an Italian priest, an expert in black magic, Gilles procured, sexually abused, and murdered over one hundred children.

When the law caught up with Gilles in 1440, not even his fortune could save him. Brought before both ecclesiastical and secular courts, he was condemned on charges of invocation of demons, human sacrifice to devils, sexual perversion, and more.[11] While many of the lurid charges made in witchcraft trials tell us more about the imaginations of the prosecutors than the activities of the accused, in Gilles' case one must acknowledge that even his confession, with its references to sadistic torture and Devil worship, may not have done justice to his activities in the ten years after he left Joan's service. And yet, during this period, this incomprehensible man took part for almost a year in a pageant-play staged at Orléans to celebrate Joan's victories. His story underlines the fact that the rise of belief in witchcraft, far from being confined to an intensification of superstition among commoners, occurred also among the ruling class, who not only feared witchcraft, but even practised it.[12]

***

The growing fear of diabolic witchcraft in the European mind strongly affected the way in which Joan was perceived. The enemies'

11. Lea, *Inquisition* 3:468-489; Georges Bataille, ed., *Le procès de Gilles de Rais: Les documents* (Paris, 1965).

12. Charles constantly consulted astrologers and retained one in his household. Joan had been approved by the seer who was resident at the time she arrived at the Dauphin's court, a fact that may have weighed in her favor as much as her endorsement by the theologians at Poitiers. Charles was so under the sway of seers that his leading theologian, Jean Gerson, felt it necessary to engage in some predictions of his own; he warned the Dauphin against spiritual seduction by 'a strange woman' who might claim to know the future and to perform wonders. Even so, when Joan appeared with her secret sign, Charles ignored Gerson's warning and let himself go along with her, and for a while at least he accepted her shamanic calling. The passion of Charles for the occult was shared by many members of his court and was part and parcel of their tendency to believe in witchcraft, to fear its power over them. That the Armagnac court accepted Joan as a seer became part of her undoing, for the line between astrology and prophecy on the one hand and sorcery on the other was thin and was becoming thinner. See Vale, *Charles VII*, pp. 43-44, 47.

highly charged fears of her virginity combined with the increasing paranoia about women as witches to create a demonic image of Joan. It was as if Joan came ready-made, or perhaps self-made, as a virginal woman onto whom her contemporaries might project the whole range of their fascinations and fears about women's sexuality. The same stories that inspired the Armagnacs served the English as proof of her diabolic power; the Duke of Alencon's confession is a case in point.

When the Dauphin's soldiers, as we have seen, came into close contact with Joan, they were rendered impotent. Even the Duke of Alencon, Joan's favorite of the nobles, confessed that when he "lay down to sleep with [her] and the soliders, all in the straw together, sometimes I saw Joan prepare for the night and sometimes I looked at her breasts which were beautiful, and yet I never had carnal desire for her...."[13] Yet while the Armagnac army interpreted this as proof of purity, her enemies used it immediately as a sign of sorcery. Because inflicting male impotency was one of the more frequent charges against witches, the English were quick to call her a follower of the Devil.

A striking piece of evidence about how Joan was perceived as witch comes from no less an authority than Jean Graverent, the grand inquisitor of France. Preaching in Paris on July 4, 1431, five weeks after Joan's burning, he made her supposed evils the centerpiece of his sermon, and in his utterance her life took on a strange shape.[14] He claimed that her parents had wanted to kill her for wearing men's clothes but were afraid to; that she had left her parents in the devil's company, and ever since had been a murderer of Christian people, full of blood and fire; that in prison, where "she was waited on like a lady," the devil, afraid that he was losing her, came in the shape of three saints to convince her to put on men's clothes again, for which she had been condemned to death; that she had called on her devils as she was dying but not one of them came.

---

13. Pernoud, *Joan of Arc*, p. 63, based on testimony given at the retrial.

14. Bourgeois, pp. 264-265. Champion's description of the sermon Graverent preached makes the identification of the inquisitor possible; see Barrett, p. 408. Noël Valois discovered a somewhat similar sermon preached in Paris against Joan, but delivered probably a few months earlier. It refers to Joan in the present, and dwells mainly on "sixty-six charges," which must be the seventy charges in circulation during the spring of the trial. This preacher's main warning was against a "cult of Joan," against her being venerated, a practice for which he gives considerable evidence: Noël Valois, "Un nouveau témoinage sur Jeanne d'Arc," *L'annuaire–Bulletin de la société de l'histoire de France* 1906 (Paris, 1907).

What was even more frightening, the inquisitor told his congregation, was that there were four such women: Joan, Catherine de la Rochelle, **Pieronne,** and a nameless companion of the latter, all of whom had been led astray by the Franciscan, Brother Richard. Three had been captured and two put to death, but Catherine remained at large. According to the sermon, Pieronne had claimed that whenever the precious body of Our Lord was consecrated she would see the great and secret wonders of Our Lord God. Implying that eucharistic visions were dangerous and stating outright that arrogant women who dress like men are servants of the devil, Graverent left no doubt in his hearers' minds about the diabolic danger of visionary women.

Graverent's sermon is like an awesome coda to Joan's end. It is like a second verdict, of the same opinion as the first, pronounced upon her dead, emphasizing her enemies' connection of her demonic power with her female gender.

To belittle the positive claims made for Joan's virginity, her anglophile judges did their best to prove that she was a whore. Article VIII of the Seventy Articles of Indictment is worth quoting in full:

> Towards her twentieth year, Jeanne, of her own wish, and without permission of her father and mother, went to Neufchâteau in Lorraine, and was in service for some time at the house of a woman, an inn-keeper named La Rousse, where lived women of evil life, and where soldiers were accustomed to lodge in great numbers. During her stay in this inn, Jeanne sometimes stayed with these evil women, sometimes took the sheep into the fields, or led the horses to watering in the meadows and pastures: it was there that she learnt to ride on horseback and to use arms.[15]

The charge, it seems, was drawn so as to imply that her whoring and her masculine ways were connected. Furthering the charge, they accused her of suing her "fiancé" for breach of promise, whereas in fact *he* had sued *her;* in the court's version, the "young man refused to marry her, because he knew she had been connected with evil women." In another Article, they charged her with having had an affair with Robert de Baudricourt, to whom they said she boasted that she would have three sons, "of whom the first should be Pope, the second Emperor, the third King," but who would be fathered not by de Baudricourt but by the Holy Spirit.[16]

15. Murray, p. 344.
16. Ibid., pp. 344-345.

Apparently these stories were fabrications; Joan denied them all and they were dropped from the final summary of charges, but they show the lengths to which the English and their French hirelings would go to defame her sexuality. The English soldiers, who had taunted her in battle, calling her harlot, bitch, sorcerer, cow-wench, continued their lewd jeers throughout her imprisonment.[17]

Fear of Joan's gender turned easily to hatred in the minds of her enemies. A creature like her could only be less than human, a foul, monstrous deformity. The English leader Bedford referred to her as:

> that disorderly and deformed travesty of a woman, who dresses like a man, whose life is dissolute....[18]

Worth pondering is the fact that none of Joan's suspicious, sorceress-like behavior seemed to count as much against her as one concrete, straighforward action: her wearing of men's clothes. Neither the flow of power she had tapped through her voices nor even her highly suspect refusal to repeat the Lord's Prayer (everyone knew that a witch could not get through it correctly) seemed to threaten her judges as much as her male attire.[19] It is difficult for those of us who accept a "unisex" dress code to understand how Joan's appearance in pants infuriated the theologians.

We know that the church accepted the transvestism of certain holy women who needed to dress as men, or even to be taken for men, in order to lead a holy life. An example of the first group was the twelfth-century English recluse Christina of Markyate, who disguised herself as a man in order to escape from an unwanted betrothal. Far from being penalized for this deviance in dress, she later lived as a consecrated virgin, honored for her asceticism.[20] In

17. Pernoud, *Retrial*, p. 144; a theologian who visited her cell when she was ill abused her verbally to the point that her fever returned (Murray, p. 254, retrial testimony).

18. Quicherat 4:382.

19. On saying the Lord's Prayer: Scott, *Jeanne d'Arc*, pp. 135-137; Murray, p. 7. In his cross-cultural study of witchcraft, Alan Macfarlane observes that social deviance is the most common cause of witch accusation, whether in Tudor England or Africa today, and lists transvestism as one type of suspected non-conformity; see *Witchcraft in Tudor and Stuart England* (New York: Harper & Row, 1970), pp. 226-227. Joan was of course not the only female transvestite of her time. Claude des Armoises was another, and still others had preceeded them; see Michael Goodich, "Contours of Female Piety in Later Medieval Hagiography," *Church History* 50 (1981), p. 25, and Vern Bullough, n. 38 below.

20. *The Life of Christina of Markyate, a Twelfth-Century Recluse*, trans. C.H. Talbot (Oxford, 1959). Christina's life as a visionary recluse indicates that she was a strongly

the second group was the German saint Hildegund (d. 1188): having been instructed by an angel to wear male garb in order to enter the monastery at Schönau, she lived there in disguise until her death. Although she suffered psychological strain from her life of imposture, she persevered, and not until the monks washed her corpse did they learn that she was female. One of the miracles on which they claimed sainthood for her was that she had preserved her chastity by her transvestism.[21]

While Hildegund's story has some claim to veracity—her biography was written by a monk who knew her well—many other tales of female religious transvestites are legendary. Of the popularity of numerous such legends, John Anson concludes that because they were written by monks they answered a psycho-sexual need of male celibates, permitting the monk to fantasize the presence of a female otherwise denied to him.[22] But Joan's transvestism won her no enthusiastic support among the clergy. The contrast between her life and that of a popular legendary transvestite, Eugenia, is instructive as to why Joan's judges condemned her so severly for her male dress.[23]

Set in the early Christian period in Alexandria, the story tells of a virgin, prevented from entering a monastery because she was a woman, who adopted male dress in order to secure membership therein. Entering the monastery with her two eunuchs, Eugenia had a miraculous interview with the abbot (he knew that she was female from a dream) and then enjoyed a long career as a Christian leader (both in and out of male dress) before being accused of practicing magic, which led to her martyrdom in Rome. Eugenia survived four out of five attempts to destroy her, and reappeared after her death to announce her coming ascension.

---

male-oriented woman: forming a close friendship with one monk, she fell in love with a second, and then became so close to the abbot of the monastery where she lived that she provoked scandal and slander. But ultimately these monastic attachments protected her, and she lived to found a community of nuns, to be the subject of a biography, and to enjoy a stipend from King Henry II. See C.J. Holdsworth, "Christina of Markyate," *Medieval Women*, ed. Derek Baker (Oxford: Ecclesiastical History Society, 1978), pp. 185-204, esp. 196-201.

21. Unpublished paper by Catherine Tuggle, "The Feminine [sic] Side of Medieval Spirituality as Exhibited in the *Vitae* of S. Lutgard, S. Alice, and S. Hildegund." Her material on Hildegund is based on *De sancta Hildegunde Virgine, Acta Sanctorum* (Paris and Rome, 1867), 2 (April):778-788.

22. John Anson, "The Female Transvestite in Early Monasticism: the Origin and Development of a Motif," *Viator* 5 (1974):1-32.

23. The following passage is based on Anson, pp. 20-25.

On *her* mission Joan also dressed as a man, accompanied by soldiers temporarily made impotent, as it were, by her purity. She also had a miraculous interview with her leader, and was accused of magical acts. More relevant to our discussion, however, are the many references in both stories to the powerful chastity of the heroines. As with many transvestite religious heroines, Eugenia is presented as the model of heroic chastity. Eugenia's virginity enabled her to effect miraculous cures, while Joan's was seen as nothing less than the surety for France's survival. But the parallels end there. Joan differed from these transvestite heroines, both legendary and actual, because she neither entered a monastery nor placed herself under the guidance of a priest. The transvestite female, or for that matter any virginal female, was acceptable only if she was under the control of the priesthood. As an independent, lay virgin wearing male clothing, Joan could be viewed as abnormal.

The monastic authors of Eugenia's legend also showed ambivalence toward female gender. They allowed Eugenia to become a Christian leader only by "acting the part of a man, by behaving with manliness, by boldly embracing the chastity which is alone Christ."[24] Her legend gives evidence of the mutually conflicting values which Christianity found in womanhood, holding it in adulation (as in the praise of motherhood and the cult of the Virgin) while also finding it something to be overcome if a woman was to achieve true heroic stature.

At best, Joan's femaleness was seen as a fact of nature which she had overcome. When an historian who wrote immediately after her death tried to praise her, he could do so only in the misogynous terms of his times. Writing that Joan had "purity of life and holiness, and neither acted as women do, nor talked as women do,"[25] he implied that women's actions were not to be trusted nor their words taken seriously.

Joan's judges resented and suspected her quickness of mind. One commented that "she was very subtle with the subtlety of a woman." Another, who began to praise her but could not forbear diluting his remarks with contempt, opined that "she answered well, notwithstanding the fragility of woman."[26]

We have seen that Joan's claims to be the special, salvific virgin and her followers' additions to that legend became charges of witch-

24. Ibid., p. 23.
25. A paraphrase from Robert Gaguin, found in *The First Biography of Joan of Arc* [written about 1500], trans. D. Rankin and C. Quintal (Pittsburg: University of Pittsburg Press, 1964), p. 35.
26. Quicherat, 2:21, 358.

craft in her enemies' hands. The ambiguous nature of her sexuality, however, was an even more damaging matter. Medieval thought was not weak in its ability to dichotomize: not least among the familiar polarities of Mary/Eve, saint/heretic, virgin/whore, was that of man/woman. The church did not want these categories blurred; as for gender, it held that a woman must be either a holy virgin or a mother, must live under the rule of a man, whether priest or husband, must in effect be married either to Christ or to an earthly spouse. Joan challenged all of these standards. Not only by her status as a single lay woman, but even more by her transvestism, close association with men, success in a man's world, and overwhelming independence of mind and action, she transgressed the accepted canons of womanly behavior.

By blurring her gender identity in these ways, Joan became highly suspect to her contemporaries. Neither Armagnacs nor English could rest until they had had Joan's body examined to see if she was a virgin, but they sought to find out more: unable to imagine that a powerful war leader was female, they thirsted to know "whether she was man or woman." Doubting that she was female, their minds lusted to know whether she was a normal specimen of either sex. One bit of hearsay from the retrial, for example, led to the assumption that Joan never menstruated: her squire reported that "many women" who had seen Joan undressed "could never learn anything [about her periods] from her clothes or in any other way."[27] The question as to whether so powerful a woman could be normal haunted both her admirers and her foes.

Even in death, Joan had to endure the indignity of being thought a freak: the executioner took care to display her body before it had burned entirely, to show "her naked body to all the people, and all the secrets that could or should belong to a woman, to take away any doubts from people's minds." When the crowd had satisfied its

27. Ayroles 4:215. Many examples of cross-dressing can be found in the literature on shamanism. For example, several parallels associated with gender blurring are apparent in the career of another charismatic woman, Kitamura Sayo, founder of Odoru Shukyo, the "dancing religion," one of numerous new religions in Japan. When Kitamura, an uneducated farmer's wife, was forty-four (in 1944) she was possessed by a female-male Shinto god, who by entering Kitamura's body created a trinity; thereafter she wore male clothing. This spirit enabled her to make invariably accurate weather forecasts, and spoke to her through a ringing sound. Ordering her to refuse to comply with certain government laws, the voice gave her the gift of ecstatic dancing and preaching, which brought her many followers. Speaking at the time of Japan's great crisis in 1945, she stood against institutional religion and priesthood, and was imprisoned for non-cooperation with the government. See Harry Thomsen, *The New Religions of Japan* (Tokyo: Charles E. Tuttle Co., 1963), pp. 199-219.

curiosity, he "got a big fire going again around her poor carcass, which was soon burned up, both flesh and bone reduced to ashes." The rumor went around that after her body was incinerated her heart remained "whole and bleeding." Lest her ashes be used to perform maleficium, they were scattered in the Seine.[28] Joan has no tomb, no relics.

Other female religious leaders have had their sexual normality or even their gender questioned. Anne Hutchinson was said to have given birth to monsters, Mother Ann Lee was stripped naked by a crowd in Massachusetts to find out if she was in fact female, and Sojourner Truth bared her breasts to the audience that taunted her for daring to speak when only men were allowed to do that.[29]

We are not less prurient today. For example, the endocrinologist Robert Greenblatt is convinced that Joan suffered from "testicular feminization syndrome" and was in fact a genetic male.[30] None of the fifteenth-century beliefs about her magical body—neither her unburnable heart nor her unassailable virginity nor her failure to menstruate—none of these speculations making Joan into an oddity, even a monster, compares with this attempt by a modern scientist to make her a male, and a defective male at that.

The basis of our own estimation of Joan's accomplishments has not changed since her time, for it still rests strongly on the perception of her overcoming the handicaps of her sex. As Carolyn Heilbrun has observed, George Bernard Shaw's Saint Joan is a hero precisely because she is "the person of no apparent importance from whom heroism...could not logically be expected," the peasant girl who could expect fame from neither her class nor her gender. When Heilbrun points out, however, that Shaw has "portrayed in one person a female being with masculine aptitudes who, in her saint-hood, reminded humanity of the need for feminine impulses in the world," she expresses a twentieth-century appreciation that would have confused Joan's contemporaries, and her positive conclusion

28. Bourgeois, pp. 263-264. The comment about Joan's heart was reported at the retrial: Murray, p. 207; about her ashes, pp. 301, 302, 305.

29. *Anne Hutchinson: Troubler of the Puritan Zion*, ed. Francis J. Bremer (Huntington, N.Y.: Krieger Publishing Co., 1981), pp. 51-71; "Ann Lee," by Susan Setta, *Women's Caucus–Religious Studies Newsletter* 5, no. 1 (Summer 1978):1; "Sojourner Truth," by Susan Setta and David J. Smucker, ibid.

30. Dr. Robert Greenblatt, article in the *Journal of Sexual Medicine*, as reported in *Omni* (April 1982), p. 102. Because of an enzyme deficiency which prevents the male organs from receiving testosterone, the principal male hormone, such genetic males "look and think like females;" they have a vagina but no ovaries or uterus. Just how Greenblatt knows how "females think" must remain as much a mystery as how he knows that Joan had no pubic hair.

that "Joan is an entirely androgynous figure,"[31] sums up what most repelled them about Joan.

It was this androgynous omnicompetence which frightened, threatened, and angered Joan's fifteenth-century enemies. Today we may admire androgyny as an ideal, as a way out of the gender trap in which both men and women find themselves. To Joan's contemporaries, the androgynous image which she had carefully composed seemed totally unnatural, a final proof of her possession by the devil.

Because Joan's society was not entirely sure whether a woman could properly be powerful, because they debated the issue, this very uncertainty made their fear of a woman who challenged the norm all the greater. There were arguments on the side of women. Archbishop Gelu, the Armagnac prelate who endorsed Joan as early as May, 1429, argued that it was credible that God would send aid to France through a woman, even one "bred on a dunghill." The very lowliness of both her gender and her social class served Gelu as an instrument to shame those lukewarm aristocrats whom he saw as stones around the king's neck. Gelu concluded by advising that, while the king must rely on himself for all practical aid, such as money, troops, and arms, he must listen to Joan on great decisions of strategy and tactics, for God would speak to him through this meritorious virgin.[32]

A second theological endorsement of Joan was more guarded. Jean Gerson said that the Maid's actions merited endorsement because she was clairvoyant and performed miracles, did not ask for money, and besides, is Christ not still with us, working for us through various means. Furthermore, she had led a pure life and, most telling, had brought about the surrender of cities. Gerson was not one to argue with that! Although morality instructed us that women must not wear men's clothes, Gerson added, still, if it was necessary in order to wage a just war, then it must be allowed.[33]

These somewhat lukewarm approbations by Gelu and Gerson are pale compared to what was written by Christine de Pisan, who

31. Carolyn Heilbrun, *Toward a Recognition of Androgyny* (New York: Knopf, 1973), pp. 110-111.

32. One is hard put to imagine what the archbishop meant by "great decisions," since Joan appears to have known nothing about technical military matters; perhaps Gelu had in mind Joan's determination not to compromise with the English. Ayroles 1:40-52; Gelu's treatise is summarized by Lucien Fabre in *Joan of Arc*, trans. G. Hopkins, Appendix II, pp. 347-348.

33. See my Appendix A for an English translation; the Latin text of *De quadam Puella* is in Dorothy G. Wayman's "The Chancellor and Jeanne d'Arc," pp. 273-305; see also Fraioli, "The Literary Image of Joan of Arc," pp. 813-815.

praised Joan unequivocally as an heroic woman and made no apology for the "weakness" of Joan's sex.[34] Christine's, however, was far from the general opinion, as we shall see. Joan's enemies judged her transvestism, her success with the army, and her sharp, spirited answers to her judges as unwomanly. Having the temerity to give her own definition of the church, rejecting the medieval church's authority in the process, she appeared to them as worse than any male heretic. That a woman was so powerful meant that she must be a deviant female–in fact, demonic.

The presence of the Devil, active and at large in Christian society, was the nightmare which had begun to haunt the dreams of the European ruling class. The Devil, loose, stood for both spiritual and political disorder, for heresy in the church, black magic in the villages, and the threat of revolution against the governments. Was not the great Hussite uprising proof enough of what could happen when people's religious beliefs became heterodox? Unthinkable disorder was sure to follow, in every aspect of social life. The prime image for this disorder was the woman-out-of-order, the "woman on top," as Natalie Z. Davis describes her, the woman who shapes history rather than submitting to the control of men.[35] As Davis discusses the horror with which sex-role reversal was greeted in sixteenth-century Europe, so Linda Nochlin reminds us that the sixteenth-century artist Pieter Brueghel, to signify the utter horror of wartime anarchy and chaos, chose for his image of spiritual and political disorder a powerful woman, "Mad Meg," who led an army during the German Peasants' War.[36] How better to show the ruin of social order than through the destructiveness of unleashed female anger?

In Joan's time and in Brueghel's, not to speak of our own, the active woman was deeply feared. Gender jealousy, or, as W.S. Scott describes it, "the dread of a woman taking the place reserved in the cultural pattern for men,"[37] is a fundamental jealousy. As a woman wearing battle dress, Joan threatened men on their own ground. As

34. Christine de Pisan, *Ditié*, stanzas 24-28 (pp. 44-45), 34-35 (p. 46), 44 (p. 47).

35. Natalie Zemon Davis, "Women on Top," in *Society and Culture in Early Modern France: Eight Essays* (Palo Alto: Stanford University Press), ch. 5.

36. Linda Nochlin, "Iconography versus Ideology: Power and Powerlessness in Nineteenth-Century Images of Women," unpublished paper presented to the Columbia University Seminar on Women in Culture and Society, 1982, pp. 22-23. Nochlin traces this negative, often witch-like, image of powerful women from Brueghel through Delacroix and others to the positive image in Kathe Kollwitz's "Black Anna" series (1904), which is based on the sixteenth-century German Peasants' War, just as Brueghel's was.

37. W.S. Scott, *Jeanne d'Arc*, pp. 142-143.

Vern Bullough observed, "Unlike the other [tranvestite saints, Joan] was always recognized as a woman, and never made an effort to be other than a woman in male garb...a simple [case of] cross-dressing...." She was a woman who chose to operate on men's territory, and what was worse, she beat them at their own game. Bullough concludes that for women "to compete on masculine grounds such as warfare was simply not permitted. Such competition represented not a gain in the status of woman but a loss of status for men, since a mere woman could succeed at what they regarded as strictly male tasks."[38]

Scott further observes that gender jealousy is especially prevalent whenever a woman attempts to assert independence or, what is worse, leadership in religious matters. He concludes that women who try to break into activities previously reserved for men may receive less hostility, may even be tolerated, if they play down their sexuality, if they become neuter, as it were. Claiming that society "pushes them toward celibacy," that is, toward a style inoffensive to, not much contrasted with, the "accepted style" of the other sex, Scott believes that Joan remained a virgin for this reason.[39] An active sexuality in an active warrior-transvestite would have been too much for her fellow citizens. Joan had to sacrifice her sexuality in order to be accepted.

The largest single group in European society suspected of witchcraft were single women. The unmarried woman, be she widow, virgin, or single for whatever reason, was seen as dangerous, because she was not under the control of a man.

By adopting virginity, that sign of female independence, as her chief symbol, Joan identified herself with a frightening type of uncontained female power. At the same time she separated herself from that other, safer female prototype, the mother. Only one reference to Joan as nurturer has been found in the contemporary literature,[40] in the *Ditié* of Christine de Pisan, who wrote of the "young maiden, to whom God gives the strength and power to be the champion who casts the rebels down, and who feeds France with the sweet, nourishing milk of peace...." Perhaps aware of the strange juxtaposition of images, Christine finished the stanza with the excla-

38. Vern L. Bullough, "Transvestites in the Middle Ages," *American Journal of Sociology* 79, no. 6 (May 1974):1381-1395, esp. 1390. Alan Macfarlane observes that both in Africa today and in England in the early modern period, independent women were frequent targets of witch accusations, especially where the men were insecure; see *Witchcraft in Tudor and Stuart England*, pp. 227-228, 233.

39. Scott, *Jeanne d'Arc*, pp. 141-142.

40. Fraioli, "The Literary Image of Joan of Arc," p. 816.

mation, "here indeed is something quite extraordinary!"[41]

While Joan's contemporaries almost universally avoided identifying her with motherhood, in the nineteenth and twentieth centuries neither the church nor the French Right has been so scrupulous. One of the most popular icons connected with La Pucelle's early years is a statue of the Virgin in the crypt of the castle chapel at Vaucouleurs, before which she prayed many times before setting out on her mission.[42] (See Plate ++++). The statue, which may still be seen in the crypt, presents the Virgin as a type of "the Queen of Heaven." She is not veiled, but instead wears a crown and a facial expression that is regal and strong. What is most unusual about the Vaucouleurs image, however, is that Mary is not holding a child: there is no Jesus connected with this Virgin. And yet, upstairs in the chapel nave, in a stained glass window executed early in this century, the following scene is portrayed: Joan in the chapel crypt, kneeling before the same statue–except that here the Virgin is pictured holding the infant Christ.

When I asked the sacristan to explain the discrepancy, he replied that the statue had originally included the child but that vandals had broken it off and stolen it "shortly after Joan's time." Sufficiently mystified to study the statue again, I found that its hands have indeed been mutilated but that there is no evidence that the figure of a child was ever there; the front is entirely smooth, the lap unbroken. I can only conclude that church authorities believed that this icon, so important first to Joan and now to her legend, would be more appropriate in the traditional style of mother-and-child. Was the proud "Queen of Heaven" too independent a symbol to be associated with Joan's cult in the years when her canonization process was being launched? Is the Mary who is venerated *because she is the Mother of Christ,* and who is therefore secondary to him, the only acceptable Mary for Joan's cult?[43]

41. Christine de Pisan, *Ditié*, p. 44.

42. In the retrial testimony, Jean Lefumeux, canon of that chapel at Vaucouleurs, affirmed that he "often saw Jeanne in this Chapel:....I have also seen her in the crypt of the Chapel on her knees before the Blessed Mary, her face sometimes bent to the ground, sometimes raised to heaven" (Murray, p. 231). Today devout Christians still pray and leave petitions before the same statue at Vaucouleurs.

43. That the tide of a cult of motherhood appears to have risen belatedly around Joan's name receives further confirmation from the products of the right-wing sculptor Maxime Réal del Sarte, one of whose statues of Joan stands in the castle chapel at Vaucouleurs, while another portrays Joan as a giant mother who shields a French soldier and a mother with baby under her huge, outspread arms. Réal del Sarte was the first president of Action Française, the virulently antisemitic, monarchist, ultraconservative political party founded at the turn of this century. As

It is ironic that the French Right made Joan a symbol of the family, because Joan left her family, resolutely running away and never going back. Although when she mentioned them during the trial she spoke with affection, yet she appears never to have called on them, neither to share her fame nor to aid her in captivity. *They* followed *her*, her brothers and a cousin joining the army after she did, her father travelling to Rheims for the coronation.[44] But having vowed her virginity to God and her voices, she henceforth placed her trust and her love in her spectral companions. A loner, Joan became an extremely self-reliant woman.

Just as witch hunters persecuted single women, the French church and the French right wing of today want to contain, to control Joan, by entombing her spirit in images of mother and of family. Neither autonomous women nor free, prophetic spirits would appear to be of use in their patheon of saints.

***

If we look back at the last week of Joan's life, two things are already clear: her enemies' belief in her demonic power, and their connection of that power with her sexuality. Joan had been condemned by both the court in Rouen and the theologians at the University of Paris; all that was lacking was a confession. On Thursday, May 24, her judges, their patience to secure a confession at an end, brought her in chains to the cemetery of St.-Ouen. Forced to stand before a large crowd and listen to a sermon during which her errors were read out, Joan made a last attempt to save herself, asking for an appeal to the pope.[45] Rejecting her plea because he claimed as bishop an omnicompetence in her case,

---

Warner has noted, when the French right wing took up her cause, it made Joan, herself an outsider because of her persecution as a witch, a symbol to be used against those other persecuted outsiders, the Jews. Warner, *Joan of Arc* pp. 260-263, and Plate 42. Warner describes still another artistic horror, the statue recently erected in Joan's mother's village, showing a child-sized Joan being pushed forward by her mother and bearing the caption, "Derrière les saints cherchez leur mère," (p. 253).

44. Marot, *Joan the Good Lorrainer:* 'the cousin, a Cistercian monk, got leave to follow Joan to the army as a chaplain (p. 31); her two younger brothers joined the army, and Pierre was captured with her at Compiègne (p. 68): her father and Pierre joined her at the coronation (p. 65).

45. During the sermon she had spoken only once: when the preacher began to vilify the French king, calling him a heretic and schismatic for following Joan, she broke in, averring that "my king is the most noble Christian of all Christians!" (Scott, *Jeanne d'Arc*, pp. 113-114). That she managed still to be faithful to Charles, after his total neglect of her, seems more naive than admirable.

Cauchon began reading the final sentence. We cannot know exactly what went on in Joan's mind: the record says merely that she suddenly interrupted Cauchon and began to recant. Submitting herself to the clergy who had pronounced her revelations false, she now swore to deny her voices and to hold to whatever the church ordained. The strain of facing imminent death had broken her. Her hand guided by the preacher, she signed a written abjuration, which described her as blaspheming and despising God, practising divination, wearing dissolute and dishonest dress, and even "cruelly desiring the effusion of human blood."[46]

Joan had saved her life, but she soon learned she had exchanged death for a sentence of life imprisonment. The bailiff advised her to request an ecclesiastical jail, where she could have female attendants, but Cauchon, who was taking no chances–Joan had twice attempted escape–sent her back to the English military prison.[47] She accepted women's dress and permitted her head to be shaved.[48]

The events of the next three days and nights cannot be known with certainty. What is clear is that on Monday, May 28, word got out that Joan had resumed male attire. Knowing that she had now trapped herself, Bishop Cauchon and a squadron of priests and lords descended on her cell. Asked why she had gone back on her word, Joan replied that it was *they* who had broken *their* word:

> ...because the promise made to me has not been kept; that is to say, that I should go to Mass and should receive my Saviour and that I should be taken out of irons.[49]

She asked to be "put into a gracious prison" where she would have a woman for a companion. As long as she was among men, it was "more lawful and suitable" for her to wear male costume.[50] Cauchon, who had "heard from several persons that she had returned to her old illusions" (his spy system had not failed him),

46. Witnesses declared later that she signed a document of no more than a few lines, but the official written recantation runs for some forty lines. The first lines, up to an ominous "etcetera," have Joan confess only that she has "sinned, in falsely pretending to have had revelations and apparitions sent from God...," but the rest, possibly filled in later, would have us think that she admitted to the full recantation. For the full text, see W.S. Scott, *The Trial of Joan of Arc*, pp. 163-164.

47. Murray, pp. 211-212, evidence given at the retrial. As it was, Cauchon had to face English anger over letting her escape the death penalty; to put it plainly, the bishop still had to find a way to bring her to the stake.

48. Barrett, p. 348.

49. Murray, p. 136.

50. Ibid.

then pressed her with the damning question; "Since last Thursday [the day of her abjuration] have you heard your Voices at all?" When Joan said yes, she double-sealed her death warrant.

What lay behind these brief statements was documented more fully in the retrial testimony of three witnesses, one of whom was Joan's court-appointed confessor. All three claimed that she was sexually abused by the English guards after she recanted and resumed wearing a skirt.[51] Perhaps her keepers felt free to rape her now that she dressed like a woman, but more important to them may have been her rejection of her voices. If Joan **confessed** that her "demons" (as the English saw them) were false and illusory, then the soldiers need no longer fear them. Her body, no longer that of a sorceress but of a poor, deluded virgin, became available. Moreover, by destroying that other source of her magic, her virginity, they were helping their cause. One might say it became their patriotic duty to rape Joan of Arc. And it would be easy: she was chained to her bed.[52]

When pressed by Cauchon as to why she had denied her voices on the previous Thursday, she claimed that she had done it "for fear of the fire."[53] Reason enough, and yet her present actions would send her straight to the stake. There was no mercy, absolutely no delay of justice, for a relapsed heretic. What had happened in her cell during those three days must have been horrendous if it forced her to condemn herself. We know that five soldiers were assigned to watch her at all times, and that three remained during the night in the cell, where Joan's legs were fastened closely to a chain held to a great log, five or six feet long. Joan told Cauchon in that fateful interview, "I would rather die than be in irons!"[54] Lest there be any doubt that she knew what she was choosing, she finished by affirming, "I would rather do penance once for all–that is die–that endure any longer the suffering of a prison."[55]

We now have a reason sufficient in itself for Joan's relapse, for retracting her recantation. Horror at facing perpetual imprisonment and sexual harassment might well be stronger than fear of being burned alive. I believe, however, that Joan had a still deeper reason for choosing death, the torment she went through over breaking

51. Pernoud, *Retrial,* pp. 182-183. There is also a story purporting that Joan's guards hid her women's dress, forcing her to resume male attire: Murray, p. 174. It is possible that in this way Cauchon framed her into perjuring herself.

52. Murray, p. 174, evidence at retrial.

53. Ibid., p. 137.

54. Ibid., p. 136.

55. Ibid., p. 138.

faith with her voices.

In a final interrogation on the morning of her death, Joan reportedly made two confessions: that the angel who had presented the crown to the king was she, and that although she had indeed heard her voices, "chiefly when the bells rang for Compline or Matins," they were evil spirits who spoke to her.[56] Some witnesses, however, claimed that she withheld judgment about the voices.

One can imagine Joan's mental torture throughout this questioning: her voices had failed her; could she mitigate her sentence in any way now by denying them? This conflict over her ultimate authority must have been intensified by the test she was put to over the Sacrament. In a scene worthy of a cosmic exorcism, Joan was allowed to receive Communion at last, after requesting it in vain for many months. She confessed her sins and was ready to receive the wafer, when the priest, already holding the Consecrated Host high above her head, asked her,

Do you believe that this is the Body of Christ?

Joan's reply affirmed more than his question had demanded:

Yes, and I believe that *He alone can deliver me;* I ask that It may be administered to me. (Emphasis mine.)

Immediately after the Communion the priest pressed her again,

Do you still believe in your Voices?

I believe in God only, and will no more put faith in my Voices, for having deceived me on this point (that she would be freed).[57]

Whatever the truth of these moments may have been, they present us with a dramatic confrontation between the late medieval world's two sources of power: the Devil and God, demonic spirits and Christ. By employing the Christian magic of the Eucharistic elements to vanquish Joan's spirits, the priest could claim to have exorcised their hold over her. Because Saints Catherine, Margaret,

56. Because all of the reports came from pro-English priests, one cannot credit them fully; claiming that Joan said exactly what the English had long wanted her to say, the reports may not be reliable. They carry a certain plausibility, however, in light of her despair over not being rescued by her voices.

57. Murray, pp. 151-152; testimony of the priest Jacques Lecamus on June 7, 1431, just a week after her death.

and Michael had not been certified by the church as proper conduits for Joan's guidance, they had been branded as diabolic illusions by the church and, because they failed to deliver her, they may have been for a brief time discredited by Joan herself. The visions of one individual were no match for an inquisitional court, especially when it had an army behind it, as it so often did. The three bearers of comfort and instruction to the heroine of France became the false demons of a witch on her way to be burned.

But this was not Joan's final word. Having surely been through an agonizing debate with herself over her betrayal of her counsel, now, at the very last, she called this betrayal her "treason." Admitting that the voices had spoken to her even as she had abjured them, she lamented that she had damned herself in order to save her life.[58] But no longer. By admitting that she still listened to her voices, she had now chosen the fire.

58. Ibid., pp. 137-138.

Chapter Six
Joan's Voice in our Time

As Sanche de Gramont observed in 1969, the trial of Joan goes on. Was she a mental case or a gifted visionary? A martyr or a fraud? A liberator of her people, as the Soviet encyclopedia claims,[1] or a holy virgin, as her Roman canonization asserts? A more important question relates to time-warp: were Joan's ideas a throwback to beliefs in magic and theocracy, archaic beliefs soon to be discarded by European culture? Or was she ahead of her time, a "proto-Protestant," staking her life on her conscience, on her right to follow her inner truth? Perhaps the sharpest set of questions we can ask concerns gender: did Joan copy male patterns of success, or does her life offer women a model of autonomous female action? That all of these claims are made for her while none is adequate indicates why we cannot describe Joan to our satisfaction. The woman from Domremy continues to defy our attempts to state her meaning for us.

The ambivalence with which her own culture viewed her has haunted Joan's legend down through time. Sculptors portrayed her as heroic and manly but also as child-like, even naive, or as the Great Mother. The list of her representations is as long as it is contradictory. Playwrights and novelists have offered us the gamut from Joan-as-witch to Joan-as-perfect-innocent. True to his fervent English nationalism, Shakespeare conjured up Joan the witch; iconoclastic Voltaire created Joan the bawdy tart; romantic Schiller did not shrink from equating Joan's power with virginity, then having her lose both virginity and power when she falls in love with an English (!) soldier; Mark Twain, perhaps deliberately straining credulity more than anyone else, evoked a wonder child whose innate wisdom is greater than her elders'; and Edward Garnett, as if to atone for his compatriot Shakespeare's view, reduced Joan to "a mere slip of a girl."[2]

1. Sanche de Gramont, *The French: Portrait of A People* (New York: Putnam's, 1969), pp. 73-77.
2. Shakespeare, *Henry VI, Part 1;* Voltaire, "La Pucelle d'Orléans," in *Oeuvres complètes,* vol. 9; Schiller, "The Maiden of Orleans," trans. J.T. Krumpelmann, in Jewkes and Landfield, *Joan of Arc,* pp. 93-164; Mark Twain (Samuel Clemens), *Personal Recollections of Joan of Arc, by the Sieur Louis de Conte* (New York, 1896; London, 1922);

Nothing attests her power more than the ability of her legend to stretch, serving causes as disparate as, on the one hand, the French monarchist movement of the nineteenth century and, on the other, Shaw's individualism and the first women's movement. With some basis in history, but mostly with human imagination at work, Joan has become everything to everyone. Her figure arouses strong, and contradictory, images of woman: good girl among the peasants, curious prodigy at court, darling of the army, prophet, magical virgin, heretic, mystic, female who learned to act and talk as a man, saint, witch, whore. We feel deeply about her, and our feelings are often ambivalent.

When Shaw had Joan say, "I shall be remembered when men have forgotten where Rouen stood," he was drawing on more than her reputation for pride; Shaw's line indicates that Joan, in her uncanny, village wise-woman way, had transcended political history. While leaving her mark on the political events of her century more firmly than any other woman, she yet went beyond politics to witness to a new kind of spiritual truth. W.S. Scott is correct in saying that her judges did not know what to make of her insistence on her own religious authority; they had never before encountered a spokesperson for individual conscience.[3]

Yet it is anachronistic to call Joan a forerunner of Protestantism. She was instead a witness to that heightened individualism that runs as a subversive thread through all of Christian history. That Joan expressed, or was forced to express, this individualism in a particularly radical way was, as we have seen, the result of two circumstances of her times: the increasingly rigid definitions of faith insisted on by the late medieval church (we have seen how the inquisitor's questions forced Joan to formulate her experiences in ways she had not yet thought out) and the respect given to female visionary experience by a society which otherwise rejected the voices of women. Joan's life illumined these two facets of late medieval society more than any others. After summarizing the insights which Joan's story brings to those two areas, I will ask two questions: What did her death mean to her contemporaries, and what can her life mean for women today?

A cult began to develop around Joan's name as soon as she was put to death. Although among the ruling class few spoke or wrote

Edward Garnett, *The Trial of Jeanne d'Arc and Other Plays* (London: Jonathan Cape, 1931).

3. George Bernard Shaw, *Saint Joan* (London, 1924; Hammondsworth: Penguin Books, 1946), Epilogue, p. 178. W.S. Scott, *Jeanne d'Arc: Her Life, Her Death, and the Myth*, pp. 140-141.

about her, silenced by the hostility of the University of Paris, to the rank and file Joan, who had become a folk hero even in her lifetime, was now seen as the woman who had saved France.[4] It is not surprising that in the provinces her brothers were able to raise enthusiasm for a false Joan, and that several other impostors appeared. Joan's leadership in the army had brought physical relief to the common people wherever the English were driven back, and her victories had raised morale across a wider area. Having fitted herself so expertly into the role of shaman for the Armagnac French, she was now able in death to become the symbol of the reviving French nation.

Joan's execution, however, triggered no mass response; there were no uprisings or protest movements. In this respect as in many others Joan illumines the deep ambivalences of late medieval France toward its need for magic workers. While aristocrats as much as commoners were drawn to her for her power over events, and while Joan fulfilled the hunger of her time for evidence that God still spoke, yet both classes distrusted the very power that they admired.

Joan had had to make up for her humble origins by joining a powerful elite, that of the charismatic virgins. Her society's willingness to accept her despite her inappropriateness for the role of military hero emphasized that they would accept a long-shot candidate, provided she could prove one thing, her connection with the spirit world. The ambivalence shows up, however, over just that point. Never entirely sure whether spiritual power was benign or demonic, they feared the very magic that they had long depended on. Just as they had shown a deep need for inspired workers, now they were on the eve of a major persecution of those same helpers.

The search for scapegoats is a theme that haunts much of Europe's history in the late middle ages; this is the obverse of the dependence on the inspired leader. Early European society was remarkably tolerant, but from the eleventh century on, two groups, dissident Christians and Jews, bore the brunt of organized repression for the next four hundred years;[5] a psychology of scapegoating was operative throughout this entire period. The violence with which dissident groups were punished was indicative of the extremism in European thought: one was either orthodox or of the devil's party. What Malcolm Lambert calls "the inquisition mentality" dominated both ecclesiastical and lay thinking, producing heresy, even artificial

---

4. Charles W. Lightbody, *The Judgments of Joan*, pp. 79, 104-108.

5. Malcolm Lambert, *Medieval Heresy*, pp. 8-10, 24-43; Leon Poliakov, *The History of Antisemitism*, trans. Richard Howard (New York: Schocken Books, 1974).

heresy where none had been until courts manufactured it.[6]

Whatever the reasons–and this question has been but little examined by historians–the record is clear: official thinking about dissent became more defensive, monolithic, rigid, and punitive. When Joan carried out her mission, as we have seen, this inquisition mentality was just going to a new phase; witchcraft was the new target, and women were therefore more suspect by virtue of gender alone than they had been. Joan was caught in this time-warp: she chose to be a female prophet and inspired leader just as suspicion of such women was growing in official circles. When in 1472 a woman, Jeanne Hachette, led an armed group in defense of Beauvais, she did not use visions nor any magical claims to gain leadership; she did not need to, and was wise not to.[7]

This need to identify and punish a demonic enemy, to carry out sacrificial deaths of atonement for the failings and sins of the larger society, raises the question of what Joan's death meant to her contemporaries. The Burgundians had from the first seen her as a strange, obsessive woman who attached herself to an illegitimate cause. Their economic advantage lay at any rate with the English, and they were furious at Joan when she rallied the Armagnac forces. Labeling her an unnatural woman and witch, their chroniclers rejoiced in her burning.[8]

For the Burgundians and English her execution was in the long tradition of propitiatory murder, which we have seen exemplified by the prisoners ritually burned to death by the Celts and the burnings of Christian dissidents and Jews by ecclesiastical courts. Muchembled notes the ritualistic nature of witch burnings, the way those executions seemed to fulfill the communities' need to witness the destruction of evil, to see with their own eyes the terrible punishment for alleged devil worship. Did Joan's death at the stake, before a huge crowd of English and their French allies, fulfill that purpose, relieving the English of their guilt over lost battles, excusing their weakness because the witch from Lorraine, the "disciple of the feende" had used the Devil's magic against them? That they profoundly rejoiced, relieved by her destruction, is clear. For the English and Burgundians, Joan was their scapegoat.

What did her public execution mean to her followers? In fitting herself so expertly into the role of shaman for the Armagnac

6. Lambert, pp. 169-172.

7. "Jeanne Hachette," *Dictionnaire d'histoire de France* (Paris, 1981). Hachette's courage was acknowledged by Louis XI, who decreed that an annual procession should commemorate the victory, in which the women should precede the men.

8. Charles W. Lightbody, *The Judgments of Joan*, pp. 58-60.

French, Joan had qualified to perform one of the shamanic acts, to reinterpret the identity of her people. Although there is plenty of evidence that the aristocracy had by the previous century accepted that "patria" meant the realm of France, this belief had never penetrated below the nobility. To the aristocracy, "patria" had come to mean not one's village or province but the whole kingdom of France. Kantorowicz has spelled out the beliefs that were part of that patriotic package: that to die for France was martyrdom, to kill for it was a merit, not a crime, that since France was just, her enemies were a fortiore unjust and to release them from their evil was the duty of Frenchmen.[9] This Crusade mentality, however, could not stand up against France's steady defeats in the Hundred Years' War, was demolished by the civil war, and had never, at any rate, been accepted by the peasantry. It was Joan, a woman of the people, who, by upgrading Charles' civil war into a holy war, reinstated the ideal of "the holy realm of France" among royalty and, more important, established it for the first time among the people.

Given Joan's role as a national hero, the further question is whether she was seen as a martyr, as one who had chosen to die for her beliefs and her cause. Her judges had set her up for the role of martyr by focusing on the issue of heresy, which is, after all, a matter of belief. But Joan never spoke of taking the role of martyr, never prophesied that she would die for France. On the contrary, she predicted until the final week that she would be rescued, and appeared to have had no ambition towards martyrdom. But the issue remains whether the Armagnacs perceived her death as a sacrifice to their cause. Evidence for popular enthusiasm for Joan is found in the response to the false Joans, the mystery play celebrating her victories, which was performed continuously at Orléans for several years after her death, and the willingness of over a hundred witnesses to come forth on her behalf at the retrial in 1455-1456. A recent interpreter of these responses to Joan, Charles Lightbody, observes that reopening Joan's case was a challenge to both the University of Paris and the inquisition, and concludes that the decision in favor of Joan broke the authority of the inquisition in France. By showing it to be inimical to the interests of the French monarchy, the retrial discredited the inquisition in the eyes of the people of France,[10] and also opened the way for seeing Joan as a national martyr.

9. Ernst Kantorowicz, *The King's Two Bodies: A Study in Medieval Political Theory* (Princeton: Princeton University Press, 1957), pp. 249-258.
10. Lightbody, *The Judgments of Joan*, p. 125.

Death as a martyr for the French laid the foundation for many unfortunate interpretations of her, in which Joan the innocent victim became all too easily the naive, pure child with no will or intelligence of her own. A number of literary works that are obsessive about Joan's death are mentioned in Nathan Edelman's account of French seventeenth-century images of La Pucelle. He tells us that the dramatist François Hédelin, for example, did not allow Joan a will of her own, having her death by burning announced by an angel at the opening of the tragedy, therefore placing the story in the context of a predestined martyrdom. Madeleine de Scudéry, writing to a correspondent, insisted that Joan was a martyr but granted Joan a bit of motivation, claiming that she did not die for the faith but "pour soutenir sa mission." An extreme example appears in Chapelain's endless epic, *La Pucelle*, where Joan rejoices when an angel tells her that heaven demands her death; she rejoices because she wants to be like Jesus, and to atone for the sins of France and of Charles VII by her suffering.[11]

The importance of the question of martyrdom for the seventeenth century's estimation of Joan is proved by Edelman's conclusion. Maintaining that its most potent image of a hero was a combination of national hero and manly knight, Edelman points out that its greatest heroes played both these roles. Two of them, Charlemagne and the crusader king St. Louis, did so; the third, however, was Joan of Arc, who could not be seen as a manly knight. She managed still to qualify, however, by adding to her role as national hero that of martyr.[12] Just as the heroines of epic and tragedy, unlike heroes, earned fame by being self-sacrificing victims who acquire knowledge passively, so Joan's reputation grew because of her sacrifice and her mysticism. But the typical heroine of epic manages to survive catastrophe, whereas in Joan's real world of warfare and inquisition, the heroine did not survive.[13]

The Joan I have described would wear the crown of martyrdom uneasily, and the trappings of sainthood even less.[14] These qualities

11. Nathan Edelman, *Attitudes of Seventeenth-Century France toward the Middle Ages* (New York: Columbia University Press, 1946), pp. 245-276. Hédelin, *Pucelle d'Orléans* (1642); Madeleine de Scudéry, in *Un tournoi de trois pucelles en l'honneur de Jeanne d'Arc* (c. 1646); Chapelain, *La Pucelle* (1656), discussed in Edelman, pp. 260-263, 273. See pp. 263-264 for reference to several seventeenth-century churchmen who requested that Joan be named a martyr of the church, and several other dramatists and antiquarians who declared that she was a saint and martyr.

12. Ibid., pp. 275-276.

13. Cf. Mary Lefkowitz, *Heroines and Hysterics* (New York: St. Martin's Press, 1981), chapters on "Women's Heroism" and "Patterns of Women's Lives in Myth."

14. Michelet, *Histoire de France*, vol. 5, bok. 10; see Egide Jeanné, *L'image de la*

of the sacrificed hero are all wrong for Joan—they have been foisted on her by our identification of her with the church, the very institution which in her lifetime rejected her and put her to death. Interpretations of Joan as "a good Catholic" all fail at this point.[15] While in her own eyes she was a good Catholic, the church itself did not agree, and many of her contemporaries seem to have been unsure about whether her faith was orthodox.

It has been observed that Western society prefers its heroes dead, and that most of its heroes are killed when they are young.[16] Joan qualified on both counts to be our heroine, but again we are not looking at the facts of her life. What are we avoiding by this mythologizing? We are refusing to look at those discomforting aspects of her life, those qualities of Joan's that do not fit our image of heroine. Joan alive, the impertinent, strong-willed boaster, who destroys our image of the saintly lady; Joan the androgynous, the transvestite, who disturbs our expectations of what female or male should be; Joan the loser, whose failures (in her own eyes) outweighed her successes, in over her head when court politics turned against her; Joan the loner, so strong in her convictions that we are offended by her self-righteousness. Who was she to think that only she could save France? No, history has preferred Joan, as its other heroes, dead, and has embellished her death with martyrdom. And that she was dead by nineteen is a definite advantage to her reputation—seen as innocent and dependent as a child, unstained by sex or worldly ambition, she can be romanticized.

***

After surveying two hundred years of historical interpretation of Joan, Egide Jeanné concluded that she cannot be studied objectively; the story is too powerful.[17] One asks therefore at one's risk what Joan's life can mean for women today. It is immediately clear that she is as controversial today as she ever has been. Her mystical

Pucelle d'Orléans dans la littérature historique française depuis Voltaire (Liège, 1935), for the criticism that Michelet defines Joan only in terms of her capacity to suffer and die (chap. 4, esp. pp. 74-75).

15. Henri Wallon in the late nineteenth century and Charles Péguy in the early twentieth are examples of the identification of Joan with Roman Catholicism; Péguy made the astonishing claim that Joan saw her mission as the saving of souls *(The Mystery of the Charity of Joan of Arc*, p. 24). See Jeanné, *L'image de la Pucelle*, chaps. 7 and 10.

16. Warner, *Joan of Arc*, p. 273.

17. Jeanné, *L'image de la Pucelle*, p. 56.

experiences continue to divide feminist opinion. Happily, there is evidence that some feminist writers today are drawn to mysticism; Susan Griffin, Margaret Atwood, Audre Lorde are examples, and their lead may indicate a need among women thinkers to push beyond the narrower canons of Western rationalism. In this respect, Joan's experience may become more available to feminist minds. On the other hand, in a time of growing repugnance at the power of the military some of us find Joan's passion for a martial career a continuing obstacle.

We should not take it for granted, moreover, that we affirm her extraordinary independence. I am suggesting that women today, while claiming greater self-determination, nonetheless feel ambivalent about their new roles. The self-direction that Joan established through the medium of her voices is threatening to contemplate; we may well ask if we want that kind of radical autonomy. And the fact that she was punished for her independence by death is appalling to women who are understandably angry at the price they are paying to live their own truth. A sampling of what women have written about Joan will indicate the degree of both their identification with and ambivalence about her life.

Long before the first, nineteenth-century women's movement there were proto-feminist voices which praised Joan's courage and accomplishments *as a woman*. In addition to Christine de Pisan's *Ditié* of 1429, there was an early popular work, the *Mirouer des femmes vertueuses* of 1546, which offered two models of female excellence: Griselda, the gentle, patient woman–and Jeanne d'Arc. Joan's valour is praised, her battles enumerated, her miraculous abilities acknowledged. This and other edifying tales kept Joan's memory alive among the people through the early modern centuries.[18]

About a century later Madeleine de Scudéry, in the course of defending Joan's reputation as a virgin, also spoke up for her choice of male clothing, maintaining that God sometimes chooses women to lead armies, that heroism is not foreign to them, witness Deborah and Judith. De Scudéry somewhat blunts this encomium by insisting that Joan had not wanted to be a military hero, that God had forced this on her, but basically she presents an heroic Joan.[19] And in the same era, under the ringing title, *Les dames illustrés où par bonnes et fortes raisons il se prouve que le sexe féminin surpasse en toutes sortes de*

18. Edelman, *Attitudes of Seventeenth-Century France*, pp. 248-249, 254. While the author of the *Mirouer* is anonymous, and therefore of unknown gender, we know that it was written for women; I include it for that reason.

19. Ibid., pp. 261-262.

genres le sexe masculin, Jacquette Guillaume declared that Joan was both a saint and a heroine.[20]

Shortly after feminist writing began to increase at the end of the eighteenth century, an eloquent feminist appraisal of Joan appeared in George Ann Grave's introduction to her English translation of Lenglet du Fresnoy's *Memoirs of Joan d'Arc* (1812).[21] **Grave argued** that Joan's intelligence, courage, and skills were real. There was nothing mysterious about them; women as well as men are capable of these accomplishments, and are equally inspired by patriotism and heroism. Claiming that "the soul is of no sex," Grave insisted that action and courage are compatible with "the milder graces and the finer feelings of humanity." Above all, she saw Joan as a real woman, as a model for other women: "The merits and glories of Joan, though extraordinary, are neither marvelous nor unnatural."[22]

But there is another school of thought among women about Joan. Believers in "true womanhood" were challenged by the first women's movement to restate their own female ideals. In rising to defend the traditional image of woman, conservative women invoked Joan's memory on their behalf. A Roman Catholic treatise praised Joan's "gentle unassertiveness," her pious childhood, and especially her ability to spin.[23] It contrasts Joan's sacrifice with the selfishness of modern women "who want victory not for their country or for God's cause but for a more selfish motive" (i.e., self-assertion), and admires her for avoiding sex. In maintaining that women's place is in the home, it appears to have wandered far from the actual life of Joan of Arc, but no, in an astonishing turn-about, it declares that Joan can still be the model for traditional Catholic women because she is the exception to this dictum; Joan qualifies because she was commanded by God to enter public life.

Making Joan a special case of course puts her on a pedestal, makes her more a miracle than a model. It ignores Joan's very real struggles to be heard and blurs her image with that of other, more pious, obedient women. It is not surprising that this article ends by paying

20. Ibid., p. 264.

21. Abbé Lenglet du Fresnoy, *Memoirs of Joan d'Arc, or du Lys, The Maid of Orléans* (Amsterdam, 1775; London, 1812), trans. George Ann Grave, with a preface, introduction, appendix and notes by the translator. My thanks to Carol Duncan for bringing this work to my attention.

22. Ibid., from George Ann Grave's preface, vi-vii, and Supplementary Remarks, pp. 150-151, 158.

23. Isabel M. O'Reilly, "The Maid of Orleans and the New Womanhood," *American Catholic Quarterly Review,* 19.75 (July, 1894):582-606. My thanks to Carol Duncan for this reference.

homage to Joan the martyr and by co-opting her and her accomplishments for the greater glory of the church. I am reminded of the present-day woman who, although she does not believe in the priesthood for women, became ordained because God willed that *she* should be a priest.

But at the same time some women were turning to Joan for very different reasons. French patriots and Catholic apologists may prefer Joan as a martyr, but feminists do not. It is Joan the powerful visionary, not Joan the martyr, who was invoked at the Seneca Falls convention in 1848 when the first call for women's suffrage was made. There Elizabeth Cady Stanton used Joan of Arc to illustrate several points basic to her feminist analysis. Observing that white men do not object to women or blacks appearing in public provided they are there to serve them, Stanton asked by way of contrast, "What man or woman has a feeling of disapproval in reading the history of Joan of Arc? The sympathies of every heart are at once enlisted in the success of that extraordinary girl." Adopting Joan's mysticism to her own reformist faith, Stanton noted that "...when all human power seemed unavailing, the French no longer despised the supernatural aid of the damsel of Domremy," and called on reform-minded women to adapt Joan's strategy to attack their own problems:

"Voices" were the visitors and advisors of Joan of Arc. Do not "voices" come to us daily from the haunts of poverty, sorrow, degradation and despair, already too long unheeded? Now is the time for the women of this country, if they would save our free institutions, to defend the right....

Exhorting her audience that "the same religious enthusiasm that nerved Joan of Arc to her work nerves us to ours," Stanton warned that the path to reform would not be easy, concluding that women when fired with a prophetic spirit would defeat those entrenched behind the bulwarks of custom and authority.[24]

In similar vein, Protestant women appealing for the right to control their own missionary work invoked "the voice, like that which followed Joan of Arc" in claiming their own "providential openings and leadings."[25] And Roman Catholic women in their

24. *Address of Elizabeth Cady Stanton Delivered at Seneca Falls and Rochester, New York, July 19 and August 2, 1848* (New York: Robert J. Johnston, 1870). I owe this reference to Mary Pellauer.

25. "Memorial Address" to the General Conference of the United Brethren in Christ, 1877, by Mrs. D.L. Rike, in *Faith that Achieved: A History of the Women's*

earliest organized demands for equal rights named their group the St. Joan's International Alliance.[26]

And yet the second women's movement itself, that phenomenon which began in the United States in the mid-1960s and has spread to many parts of the world, has not utilized Joan's life as one of its models. A look at what one of its leading theoreticians has written about her may explain why. Opining that "Joan of Arc's adventure...was only a brief escapade," Simone de Beauvoir concluded that "most female heroines are oddities...if we compare Joan of Arc, Mme. Roland, Flora Tristan, with Richelieu, Danton, Lenin, we see that their greatness is primarily subjective: they are exemplary figures rather than historical agents." Not only does de Beauvoir go against the grain of almost all recent appraisals of Joan in denying that she was an historical agent, she further misses the mark in applying a narrowly androcentric definition of what heroism is. If heroism is best exemplified by Richelieu, Danton, and Lenin, we may fairly ask for a broader definition of historical greatness. De Beauvoir's penchant for assuming a male standard, even while writing sympathetically about women, distorts her appreciation of Joan.

Although de Beauvoir's thesis is precisely that it is male control of society which keeps women from acting as historical agents, still she herself is slow to observe when a woman manages to act on her own. Complaining that history offers us many male heroes, "so many men for one Joan of Arc;" she then disqualifies even Joan by complaining that "behind her one descries the great male figure of the archangel Michael!"[27] She thereby ignores Joan's testimony that it was St. Catherine who appeared to her most often, not that "great male figure." Assessing Catherine of Siena's career as more successful and more self-directed than Joan's, de Beauvoir strangely prefers Catherine of Siena's failures as a political negotiator to Joan's success in turning the tide of the Hundred Years' War. So too did courts of the fifteenth-century Roman Church assess these two, awarding Catherine sainthood and condemning Joan to death.

De Beauvoir's own insights might have taught her better: she knew the difference between narcissistic and active mysticism, and between true heroism and feigned sacrifice, brilliantly analyzing the

Missionary Association of the Church of the United Brethren in Christ, 1872-1946, by Mary R. Hough (Dayton, Ohio, 1958). My thanks to Hilah Thomas for this reference.

26. *NCE*, vol. 12. The Alliance was founded in London in 1911.

27. Simone de Beauvoir, *The Second Sex*, trans. and ed. H.M. Parshley (New York: Bantam Books, 1952), pp. 96, 121-122, 269.

masochism and sadism in those who merely "play the martyr."[28] Observing that Joan of Arc, as well as Theresa of Avila and Catherine of Siena, were strongly self-directed women, she acknowledges that women are nonetheless never free, for "the Church sees to it that God never authorizes women to escape male guardianship; she has put exclusively in man's hands such powerful weapons as excommunication; obstinately true to her visions, Joan of Arc was burned at the stake."[29]

But after this apt observation de Beauvoir does not ask why Joan was punished while Theresa and Catherine of Siena were glorified; in that question, however, lies the message of Joan's life for us. The woman who recognized no masculine authority whatever, who chose no official confessor, biographer, nor order, who acted on her own and took full responsibility for her actions, and who honored her own truth above her life, received the heaviest condemnation which church and secular power could deliver. Joan's lesson for women is first to follow her example in taking themselves seriously and finding their own truth, in searching for their authentic voice, free of the definitions of male authority. But the further message of Joan's life is that women must not assume that their truth is acceptable in the world of male values.

Joan's meaning for women is therefore to be found both in her death and her life. Her death tells of punishment in store for women who dare find their own truth and live by it: female prophets were less honored in France after Joan's death. The message had been made clear: a warning to women to shut out their inner voice, to listen instead to the voices of male authority in church and society. The realism of this message is one legacy of Joan's life, which otherwise stands as a model of female self-direction.

---

28. Ibid., chap. 24, "The Mystic," and pp. 585-588.

29. Ibid., p. 586. See also p. 637, where she again includes Joan with the active mytics "who know very well what goals they have in mind and who lucidly devise means for attaining them."

Appendix

In the spring of 1429 Jean Gerson, the leading theologian loyal to the Armagnac cause, wrote a treatise about Joan, looking at arguments both for and against her, and concluded that she was to be trusted.

Gerson had been named chancellor of the University of Paris in 1395. His distinguished career had been capped by his work to end the papal schism at the Council of Constance, 1414-16, but the Council provided his last major role, for Paris was now in the hands of the Burgundians and Gerson was forced into exile. Settling eventually in Lyon, Gerson would have learned of Joan's entry into public life through his many connections among the Armagnac theologians who examined her at Chinon and Poitiers, especially the Dauphin's confessor, Gerard Machet and his ambassador to Constance, Pierre de Versailles. He must have written this tract before May 8, 1429, since he does not mention the famous victory at Orleans on that date. Gerson died soon after, on July 12, 1429. The treatise stands therefore as an early witness to Joan's mission.

The text of *De quadam puella* has had a varied history. It was first published in 1484 in the first compilation of Gerson's works.[1] But long before that, a second treatise ascribed to Gerson had appeared, *De mirabili victoria*, referred to as early as November 20, 1429, in a letter by the Venetian ambassador Justiani, who quotes verbatim from it, adding that the essay has been sent to Rome by the University of Paris in order to accuse both Joan and Gerson of heresy.[2]

That *De mirabili victoria* was important to the Burgundians is borne out by its appearance in the captured Anglo-Burgundian transcript of Joan's trial used as evidence at her retrial of 1456, where it is the only work ascribed to Gerson.[3] The identity of these two treatises becomes much more tangled with the publication of the second edition of Gerson's *Opera* in 1514.[4] Here *De quadam puella* is assigned to the Dutch canon Henry of Gorckheim, and *De mirabili victoria* is offered as Gerson's single work on Joan.

The influential Quicherat and all later editors of Gerson followed these ascriptions, except Ellies Du Pin in 1706, who had denied that either treatise was by the Chancellor.[5] On the other hand, two French Gerson scholars at the turn of this century concluded that *both* were Gerson's work. One of the scholars, Masson, analyzed *De quadam puella* at length while only mentioning the other tract,[6] whereas *De mirabili victoria* received a book-length study and French translation by J.-B. Monnoyeur in 1910.[7] Finally in 1956 *De quadam puella* was returned to Gerson's authorship by Dorothy G. Wayman, who declared it to be the *only* work of

Gerson about Joan, and separated the other tract from it and assigned it to an anonymous Burgundian cleric hostile to Gerson.[8]

Wayman's careful analysis of *De quadam puella* convincingly shows that its scholarship qualifies it as the work of the famous churchman. The definite ascription of the other treatise remains at issue and requires more work; I am not entirely convinced that Gerson did not write it also.

As one of the earliest written comments about Joan, *De quadam puella* reveals how widely she was discussed and at what high levels. Gerson's statement that cities, towns, and castles were now going over to the Dauphin's obedience (*before* Orleans) points up how swiftly she improved the Armagnac fortunes. More than that, however, it shows how controversial she was. People were already deeply concerned that the source of her power might be demonic, that she might be a sorceress, and were offended that she wore male dress. Gerson accepts the miraculous nature of her gifts and concludes that they are God-given, because she is by all reports unworldly, chaste, and not ambitious for herself. But Gerson is not entirely enthusiastic; the image of a female warrior made him uneasy.

For other positive estimates of Joan written as early as May of 1429, see *De mirabili victoria* and Archbishop Gelu's treatise.[9]

The following translation is based on the text in Wayman.

1. *Opera Gersonii*, ed. J. Koelhoff (Cologne, 1484) vol. IV. The text is available today in Quicherat, vol. III: 411-21, ascribed to Henri de Gorcum, and in Dorothy G. Wayman, "The Chancellor and Jeanne d'Arc," *Franciscan Studies*, 17 (1957): 296-305.

2. Ayroles, III: 574.

3. Quicherat, III: 298-306; available also in Wayman, where it is printed beside the text of *De quadam puella*. The next known reference to it is by Jean Bouchet, *Annales d'Aquitaine*, C. 1500, who attributes it to Gerson.

4. *Opera Gersonii*, ed. J. Knoblauch (Strasburg, 1514) vol. II.

5. Ellies Du Pin, ed. *Opera Gersonii* (Amsterdam, 1706) III: 859-64.

6. M. Masson, *Jean Gerson, sa vie, son temps, ses oeuvres* (Lyon: Vitte, 1894): 341, 384-47; Albert Lafontaine, *Jean Gerson* (Paris: Poussielque, 1906): 310-13.

7. J.-B. Monnoyeur, *Traite de Jean Gerson sur la Pucelle* (Paris: Champion, 1910).

8. See n. 1. Deborah Fraioli, "The Literary Image of Joan of Arc," *Speculum* 56:4 (1981), suggests that *De quadam puella* influenced Christine de Pisan's *Ditie*, reminding us that Gerson and Christine were friends, and pointing out that both works group Esther, Judith, and Deborah as forerunners of Joan (pp. 815-17).

9. Archbishop Jacques Gelu: Quicherat, III:393-410.

De quadam puella

A certain treatise, bringing together and comparing propositions about a certain maid who some time ago rode in France, set forth by Master Jean Gerson.

To the glory of the blessed Trinity, the glorious, ever-Virgin Mother of God, and the whole court of heaven.

"The Lord took me when I followed the flock and the Lord said unto me: 'Go, prophesy to my people Israel.'" [Amos 7:15]. Not inappropriately can the people of the kingdom of France be called the people of Israel in a spiritual sense since it is well known that they have always prospered through their faith in God and their observance of the Christian religion. To the heir of this kingdom has come a certain young girl, the daughter of a certain shepherd, who herself is said to have tended the common flock, asserting that she has been sent by God so that through her the said kingdom might be restored to his obedience. That, however, this claim of hers might not be considered rash, she also employs supernatural signs, such as revealing the secrets of hearts and foreseeing future events.

It is further reported that she has her hair cropped in the manner of a man and that eager to sally forth to military actions, she mounts her horse clad in male attire and armor. While she is on horseback carrying her banner, she is immediately infused with a miraculous activity, as if she were a general experienced in the strategic deployment of an army. At that time her men, too, become high-spirited, but her enemies, on the other hand, are as fearful as if devoid of strength. As soon as she dismounts from her horse, however, and reassumes ordinary female attire, she becomes very artless, as ignorant of worldly affairs as an innocent lamb. It is said furthermore that she lives in chastity, sobriety and moderation, devoted to God, preventing murder, pillage and other violent acts from being done in all those who are willing to behave themselves in accordance with the aforementioned obedience. For these and similar reasons, cities, towns, and castles are submitting themselves to the royal heir, pledging their fidelity to him.

Since the situation is such as has just been described, several questions arise that attract the attention of learned minds to make a statement about them. For example, whether it ought to be believed

that she is a true maid with a human nature, or something transformed into a fantastical human likeness. Second, whether what she
does could be done by her after the manner of men, or through her
by some higher power. Third, if through a higher power, whether
through a good power, namely a good spirit, or through an evil one,
an evil spirit for instance. Fourth, whether credence should be
placed in her words and whether her accomplishments should be
received with approval as if done by divine providence, or are acts of
sorcery and delusions.

Since, indeed, with respect to these and similar minor questions
some people think one way, others the opposite, in order that both
sides may cite evidence from sacred scripture for their defense, this
present work offers some propositions for one side, then some for
the other, in a problematic form of argument, not for the sake of
asserting their correctness but to bring the various arguments
together and repeat them here, challenging more subtle minds to a
more profound understanding of them. Nevertheless, by committing
to memory that which may be useful for expressing some opinion
safely in this matter, it is necessary to have beforehand a clear
understanding of the maid's habits, words, deeds, and all her other
traits, as much those she possesses while alone as those which she has
with others in public–along with other circumstances of her life. And
should the things which she reveals and foretells always be found to
be true, they ought to be accepted and regarded as true in future
according to the report of public opinion brought to these parts by
many trustworthy men.

FIRST PROPOSITION: It should be plainly stated that she is a true
maid and a real person with a human nature.

This proposition is clear because the rule of <theologians?> to
say nothing of philosophers states that deeds reveal form; indeed,
even our Saviour testifies that by their deeds you shall know them
[cf. Matt. 7:16]. Therefore, since this young girl is at all times found
to conform with other human beings in human actions by speaking,
being hungry, eating, drinking, waking, sleeping, and other activities
of this kind, who would dare to say that she is not a real person with
a human nature in respect to other similar signs of human nature
which accompany these. Therefore, etc.

SECOND PROPOSITION: The ordinary time of prophecy was
before the coming of Christ and lasted, along with the performance
of miracles, until the beginning of the newly-founded Church.

This proposition is explained by sacred teachers by the fact that the whole period of the Old Testament was prefigurative in order to foretoken the coming of Christ and the future state of His mystical body. Similarly in the primitive Church many people are said to have been prophets and because what was predicted at that time transcends all understanding by human faculties, it was necessary to add signs in the form of miraculous works by which the truth of these words might be confirmed. Otherwise the salvation of the human race would have been less than sufficiently provided for, according to the words of Gregory: that a plant newly set in the earth is in need of frequent watering, so that well rooted, it will grow strong. Therefore, etc.

THIRD PROPOSITION: In our times it is not considered unseemly that now and then certain persons be roused to the spirit of prophecy and be moved to perform miracles.

This proposition is that of Augustine in *The City of God* and is clearly drawn from the doctrine of Gregory. His statement is also clear from the fact that it has been promised to us by the word of the Saviour that He Himself is with us "even to the consummation of the world" [Matt. 28:20], directing the human race by the hand of His providence accordingly as the opportunities for our salvation provide. For just as He has not restricted His power to the sacraments neither has He restricted it to any time, places, or persons; nay rather in His many mercies He always assists the human race by providing fit remedies and aids. For, Isaiah says, "the hand of the Lord is not shortened so that it can not redeem us" [Is. 59:1]. Therefore, etc. Since therefore, the human race needs to be roused and recalled by the revelation of secrets and the performing of miracles, now among one people, now among another, the opinion must be piously expressed that such acts are not to be denied us. Therefore, etc.

FOURTH PROPOSITION: It is consonant with sacred scripture that through the frail sex and innocent youth joyful salvation has been revealed by God to people and to kingdoms.

This proposition is clear because, as the Apostle is our witness, God chooses the weak things of the world that He may confound the strong [1 Cor. 1:27], whoever they may be. Hence, proceeding by way of examples, one reads that through Deborah, Esther, and Judith deliverance was attained for God's people and that Daniel was roused in his boyhood to achieve the acquittal of Susannah [Dan.

13:45]. So too David, while still a boy, caused the downfall of Goliath. And not unjustly, because in this way the bounty of divine compassion is made more evident so that man may not ascribe these acts of grace to his own strength but rather should refer them to God. For thus through a humble virgin the redemption of all mankind came to pass. Therefore, etc.

FIFTH PROPOSITION: Holy scripture gives no evidence that men of evil life have been sent from God in such a guise or manner as general opinion attributes to the aforementioned maid.

This proposition is clearly correct because, as the Apostle says, there is "no concord between Christ and Belial" [2 Cor. 6:15], nor did He deign to enter the society of, or to contract familiarity with, demons and their ministers and members, although He may sometimes choose certain evil men to prophesy something in passing as Balaam prophesied that "a star would rise out in Jacob" [Num. 24:17] and Saul and Caiaphas also prophesied [cf. 1 Sam. 10: John 11:51]. But it is entirely different as far as this maid is concerned, she who has at her command the power of supernatural gifts to make known secret things and to foretell the future, preventing, furthermore, as has been previously mentioned, those devoted to her service from murders and other crimes being done, exhorting them to virtues and other acts of moral integrity by which God is glorified. Just so was Joseph sent ahead into Egypt before his father and brothers by the spirit of God [Gen. 45:7], and Moses to liberate the people of Israel, and Gideon and the women mentioned earlier. In the same way it is not incongruous that this young girl should be numbered among the good especially sent by God, particularly since she does not ask for any rewards but labours for the blessing of peace with total devotion. For this is not the work of an evil spirit, who is the author of dissension rather than of peace.

SIXTH PROPOSITION: It follows as a corollary from the propositions previously stated that this girl is a real person with a human nature, sent especially by God to do those deeds which are done not by her own human powers but divinely, and that trust is to be placed in her.

This proposition is clearly in agreement with the questions examined above. That she is truly a human being is clear from the first proposition, and since God has not ceased even in these days to provide specially for us through supernatural signs, it is not inappropriate for God to make use of an innocent girl, especially in view of the fourth proposition. And since this very gift remains steadfastly with her until the divinely consecrated fulfilment of His purposes through the means of virtue and honesty, as the fifth proposition asserts, it seems that this sixth proposition must consequently be conceded as well. Nor is it at all surprising that in the guise of a knight she should have quite another brilliance than in her ordinary womanly state, because even David, wishing to consult the Lord, dressed in an ephod [2 Sam. 6:14] and took up the harp, and Moses, while he carried the rod, performed miracles [Num. 20]; because, as Gregory says, the Holy Spirit frequently conforms itself within to the external shapes it comes in contact with.

Thus from what has been briefly touched on here any supporter of this way of thinking can take the opportunity of defending her side, and indeed go even further into a fuller amplification of it. But because others are found who are more inclined to the opposite side, it remains for us to produce certain witnesses from holy scripture from which they may select the supports for their position by examining the propositions set forth below.

FIRST PROPOSITION: Many false prophets will come, asserting that they have been sent from God by divine providence.

This proposition is based on the saying of the Saviour that in the last days, namely of the law of the gospel, "many will say that they come in my name" [cf. Matt. 24:5] and many will be deceived by them. Hence the Apostle says that the angel of "Satan transforms himself into an angel of light" [2 Cor. 11:14]. Nor is it surprising that that evil "king over all the sons of pride" [Job 41:25] strives incessantly to usurp the perfection of divinity. And for that reason he procures false prophets sent in God's name in order to deceive. Therefore, etc.

SECOND PROPOSITION: False prophets frequently make known publicly the secrets of hearts and the outcome of future events.

This proposition is usually conceded by learned men. The reason for this is that the more lofty a moral excellence may be the further it extends itself to greater things. It is well known, however, that the understanding of demons is superior to human understanding, and thus those things which are hidden for us and those future events which are unknown to us are known by an evil spirit.

THIRD PROPOSITION: It is not easy to distinguish a true prophet from a false one through exterior appearances and signs.

This proposition is clear because it is not necessary for a prophet to lead a virtuous life or to have grace. Demonic prophets can even know what is hidden for us and foretell future events, and this is the case with many other things in respect to which they accord with true prophets. If now and then they predict something falsely they know how to conceal their mistake by giving their prediction another meaning, or they claim that true prophets sometimes prophesy things which have not happened, as is said of the prophets Isaiah and Jonah. For this reason even the Apostle says "believe not every spirit but try them if they be of God [1 John 4:11], implying that it is hard to distinguish between good and evil prophets. Therefore, etc.

FOURTH PROPOSITION: Now in this time of grace that a special mission should be sent from God for the purpose of furthering worldly happiness does not have much appearance of plausibility.

This proposition can be assumed from what Augustine so often reminds us of: for the good things of the present life are granted equally to good and bad alike, to the just and the unjust, especially in this time of grace so that good men will not fasten their affection on transitory goods on which evil men thrive, but that rather they may concentrate on those goods which He reserves for His followers in the life to come. Since He lavishly confers the transitory goods of this life upon His enemies, a mission made to procure present happiness and to predict those things which, it is written, ought to be held in low esteem, would therefore seem to have little plausibility. Nevertheless it is written in the Old Testament how the people of Israel used to serve God for the sake of these temporal goods, and reference has sometimes been made to this fact. Therefore, etc.

FIFTH PROPOSITION: This maid commits two offences which are forbidden in holy scripture.

This proposition is clear because in Deut 22[:5] the law forbids a woman from wearing man's apparel and the Apostle forbids a woman from cutting her hair like a man's [cf. 1 Cor. 11:6]. The opposite of both these prohibitions is reported about this maid, and it seems at first glance to verge on some kind of indecency that the maid should ride on horseback clad in male attire. And since God delights in modesty, it seems to detract from her divine mission to unsex herself into a masculine appearance. Nor does such a manner appear to be consonant with her own private mission since such a private mission is made through the spirit sanctifying the soul within, according to the saying in Wisdom 7[:27-28] that the Wisdom of God "passes into holy souls and makes them friends of God and prophets." For this reason if the mission of this young girl were prophetic, it is necessary that she be of a certain outstanding holiness and of divine mind; on the other hand, it seems indecent that such a person transform herself into a secular man of arms. Not thus is it written about Esther and Judith: although they decked themselves out in very festive women's adornments, they did so nevertheless in order to be more pleasing to those whom they intended to deal with. Therefore, etc.

SIXTH PROPOSITION: It cannot be shown with sufficient plausibility that the said girl has been sent specially by God and that God works through her or that she should be trusted.

This proposition is evident as a corollary drawn from the above statements because (1) if many false prophets will come resembling true prophets; (2) if a special mission is not made to achieve prosperity of temporal happiness in this time of grace; (3) if her undertaking is done counter to divine mandates, how can it be positively held that a girl of this sort has been singularly chosen by God to achieve the ends which are reported.

From all this it is clear how the proponents of this way of thinking might colour their side of the dispute by impugning the opposite side, and by taking the opportunity offered by the above statement for finding even more profound arguments.

And so these arguments, gathered together from here and there and put down in a comparative fashion, are offered to those who will care to look at them for the sake of the present case or of a future one like it so that they may be able to respond in some way to those raising similar questions, always to the glory of God who reigns hallowed forever. Amen.

Bibliography

I. DOCUMENTS

Bourgeois of Paris. *A Parisian Journal: 1405-49*, trans. Janet Shirley, from *Le Journal d'un Bourgeois de Paris*; ed. A. Tuetey. Paris, 1881; Oxford, 1968.

de Voraigne, Jacob. *The Golden Legend*, trans. G. Ryan and H. Rippenberger. New York: Longmans, Green, & Co., 1941.

First Biography of Joan of Arc, trans. Daniel Rankin and Claire Quintal. Pittsburgh: University of Pittsburgh Press, 1964.

Gerson, Jean. "De mirabile Victoria cujusdam Puellae." In *Opera*, vol. 2. Paris, 1521; and in Quincherat, vol. 4: 298-306.

——— ."De quadam puella." In *Opera*, vol. 2. Paris, 1521. Reprinted in Dorothy G. Wayman, "The Chancellor and Jeanne d'Arc," *Franciscan Studies* 17.2-3 (June-September, 1957): 273-305. For English translation, see my Appendix A.

——— ."Tractatus ... de distinctione verarum visionum." In *Opera Omnia*. Antwerp, 1706.

Hadewijch, *The Complete Works*, trans, Columba Hart. New York: Paulist Press, 1980.

Jeanne d'Arc, Maid of Orleans: As set forth in the Original Documents, trans. T. Douglas Murray. New York: McClure, Phillips & Co., 1902.

Joan of Arc, by Herself and her Witnesses, ed. Regine Pernoud, trans. Edward Hyams. New York: Stein & Day, 1966.

Meister Eckhart. *Breakthrough: Meister Eckhart's Creation spirituality in New Translation*, ed. Matthew Fox. Garden City: Doubleday, 1980.

Mechtild of Magdeburg. *The Flowing Light of the Godhead*, trans. L. Menzies (London, 1953).

Minute français des interrogatoires de Jeanne la Pucelle, ed. P. Doncoeur and Y. Lanhers. Melun, 1956.

Pisan, Christine de. *Ditié de Jehanne d'Arc*, ed., trans. Angus J. Kennedy and Kenneth Varty. Oxford: Society for the Study of Medieval Languages and Literature, 1977.

Porete, Marguerite. *A Mirror for Simple Souls*, trans. and adapted by Charles Crawford. New York: Crossroad Publishing Co., 1981.

Procès de condemnation et de réhabilitation de Jeanne d'Arc dite la Pucelle d'Orléans, ed. Jules Quicherat, 5 vols. Paris: Renouard, 1841-49; New York: Johnson Reprint Corp., 1965.

Procès de condamnation de Jeanne d'Arc, ed. and newly annotated by Pierre Tisset and Yvonne Lanhers. 3 vols. Paris: Klincksieck, 1960, 1970-71.

Procès de Gilles de Rais: Les Documents, ed. Georges Bataille. Paris, 1965.

Réhabilitation de Jeanne la Pucelle, ed. P. Doncoeur and Y. Lanhers. Paris, 1956.

Rédaction Episcopale du Procès de 1455-56, ed. P. Doncoeur and Y. Lanhers. Paris, 1961.

Retrial of Joan of Arc, ed. Regine Pernoud, trans. J. M. Cohen. London: Methuen, 1955.

Trial of Jeanne d'Arc, with an essay by Pierre Champion, trans. W. P. Barrett. London: Gotham House, 1932.

Trial of Joan of Arc, trans. W. S. Scott. London: The Folio Society, 1956. Based on the Orleans manuscript.

Vita Sanctae Coletae (1381-1447), ed. Yves Cozaux et al. Leiden: Brill, 1982.

Teresa of Avila. *The Life*, trans. J. Cohen. London: Penguin Books, 1957.

II. JOAN'S LIFE: A SELECT LIST OF BIOGRAPHIES AND PLAYS

Ayroles, Jean Baptist J. *La vraie vie de Jeanne d'Arc*. 5 vols. Paris, 1890-1902.

Boutet de Monvel, Maurice. *Joan of Arc*, trans. A. I. du P. Coleman. Paris, 1897; New York: Viking Press, 1980. (Although written for children, the book's justly famous illustrations make it of interest to adults as well.)

Clemens, Samuel (Mark Twain). *Personal Recollections of Joan of Arc by the Sieur Louis de Conte.* London: Chatto and Windus, 1896. A fictionalized life.

Fabre, Lucien. *Joan of Arc*, trans. Gerard Hopkins. London: McGraw-Hill, 1954.

France, Anatole. *The Life of Joan of Arc*, trans. W. Stephens. Paris, 1904; London, Bodley Head, 1923.

Gies, Frances. *Joan of Arc: the Legend and the Reality.* New York: Harper & Row, 1981.

Garnett, Edward. *The Trial of Jeanne d'Arc and Other Plays.* London: Jonathan Cape.

Lang, Andrew. *The Maid of France.* London: Longmans, 1909.

Lucie-Smith, Edward. *Joan of Arc*, New York: Norton, 1976.

Michelet, Jules. *Joan of Arc.* Paris, 1853. trans. Albert Guerard. Ann Arbor: University of Michigan Press, 1957.

Sackville-West, Vita. *Saint Joan of Arc.* New York: Doubleday, 1936.

Schiller, Friedrich von. *The Maiden of Orleans*, trans. J. T. Krumpelmann in *Joan of Arc: Fact, Legend and Literature*, ed. Wilfrid T. Jewkes and Jerome B. Landfield. New York: Harcourt, Brace, 1964.

Scott, W. S. *Jeanne d'Arc: Her Life, Her Death, and the Myth.* London: Harrap & Co., 1974.

Shaw, George Bernard. *Saint Joan.* London, 1924; Hammondsworth: Penguin Books, 1946.

III. RELEVANT STUDIES OF JOAN OF ARC

Delaruelle, E. *La spiritualité de Jeanne d'Arc.* Toulouse: Bulletin de Littérature Ecclésiastique, 1964. 1 and 2.

De la Martiniere, Jules. "Frere Richard et Jeanne d'Arc à Orleans, Mars-Juillet 1430." *Le Moyen Age*, 3rd ser., vol. I (Janvier-Mars 1934): 189-98.

Fraioli, Deborah. "The Literary Image of Joan of Arc." *Speculum*, vol. 56, no. 4 (Oct. 1981): 811-830.

Guitton, Jean. *Problème et mystère de Jeanne d'Arc.* Paris: Fayard, 1961.

Ince, R.B. *Joan of Arc.* London: Wm. Rider & Son, 1921.

Jeanné, Egide. *L'Image de là Pucelle d'Orléans dans la littérature historique francaise depuis Voltaire.* Liège, 1935.

Jewkes, Wilfrid T. and Landfield, Jerome B., eds. *Joan of Arc: Fact, Legend and Literature.* New York: Harcourt, Brace, 1964.

Lenglet du Fresnoy, Abbé. *Memoirs of Joan d'Arc, or du Lys, The Maid of Orléans.* Amsterdam, 1775; London, 1812, trans. George Ann Grave, with a preface, introduction, appendix and notes by the translator.

Lightbody, Charles W. *The Judgments of Joan: A Study in Cultural History.* London: Allen and Unwin, 1961.

Marot, Pierre. *Joan the Good Lorrainer at Domremy.* Colmar: Editions S.A.E.P., 1981.

O'Reilly, Isabel M. "The Maid of Orleans and the New Womanhood," in *American Catholic Quarterly Review*, 19.75 (July 1894): 582-606.

Peguy, Charles. *The Mystery of the Charity of Joan of Arc*, trans. Julian Green. New York: Pantheon Books, 1950.

Raknem, Ingvald. *Joan of Arc in History, Legend, and Literature.* Oslo: Universitetsforlaget, 1971.

Searle, William. *The Saint and the Skeptics: Joan of Arc in the Works of Mark Twain, Anatole France, and Bernard Shaw.* Detroit, 1976.

Vale, Malcolm. "Jeanne d'Arc et ses adversaires: la victime d'une guerre civile?" Orléans: Centre National de la Récherche Scientifique, 1981.

Valois, Noel. "Jeanne d'Arc et la prophetie de Marie Robine" in *Melanges Paul Fabre.* Paris, 1902.

_____. "Un nouveau témoinage sur Jeanne d'Arc," in *L'Annuaire-Bulletin de la Société de l'Histoire de France, 1906.* Paris, 1907.

Vauchez, André. "Les Soeurs de Jeanne." *Le Monde*, January 6, 1980, pp. 15-16.

Wagenknecht, Edward, ed. *Joan of Arc: An Anthology of History and Literature.* New York: Creative Age Press, 1948.

Warner, Marina. *Joan of Arc: the Image of Female Heroism.* New York: Knopf, 1981.

Wayman, Dorothy G. "The Chancellor and Jeanne d'Arc," *Franciscan Studies* 17.2-3 (June-September 1957): 273-305.

IV. RELATED WORKS

Anson, John. "The Female Transvestite in Early Monasticism: the Origin and Development of a Motif," in *Viator* 5 (1974): 1-32.

Baker, Derek, ed. *Medieval Women*. Studies in Church History, Subsidia I. Oxford: Basil Blackwell, 1978.

Benton, John F. "Consciousness of Self and Perceptions of Individuality," in *Renaissance and Renewal in the Twelfth Century*, eds. Robert L. Benson and Giles Constable, with Carol D. Lanham. Cambridge: Harvard University Press, 1982.

Bolton, Brenda M. "Vitae Matrum: a Further Aspect of the Frauenfrage," in *Medieval Women*, ed. Derek Baker. Oxford: Basil Blackwell, 1978.

Bremer, Francis J., ed. *Anne Hutchinson: Troubler of the Puritan Zion* (Huntington: Krieger Publishing Co., 1981).

Brown, Peter. *The Cult of the Saints: Its Rise and Function in Latin Christianity*. Chicago: University of Chicago Press, 1981.

————. "Society and the Supernatural: A Medieval Change." *Daedalus* (Spring 1975): 133-51.

————. "Sorcery, Demons, and the Rise of Christianity: from Late Antiquity to the Middle Ages," in *Religion and Society in the Age of St. Augustine*, ed. Peter Brown. London: Faber and Faber, 1972.

Buggge, John. *Virginitas: the History of the Medieval Ideal*. The Hague, 1975.

Bullough, Vern L. "Transvestites in the Middle Ages," in *American Journal of Sociology* 79.6 (May, 1974): 1381-95.

Bynum, Caroline Walker. *God the Mother: Studies in the Spirituality of the High Middle Ages*. Berkeley: University of California Press, 1982.

Chaume, Maurice. "Une Prophétie Relative à Charles VI" in *Révue du Moyen Age Latin*, Vol. III (1947): 27-42.

Christian, William A., Jr. *Apparitions in Late Medieval and Renaissance Spain*. Princeton: Princeton University Press, 1981.

Cohn, Norman. *The Pursuit of the Millenium*, rev. ed. New York: Oxford University Press, 1970.

Cuming, G. J. and Baker, Derek, eds. *Popular Beliefs and Practice*. Cambridge: Cambridge University Press, 1972.

Cunliffe, Barry. *The Celtic World*. New York: McGraw-Hill, 1979.

Davis, Michael. *William Blake: A New Kind of Man*. Berkeley: University of California Press, 1977.

Davis, Natalie Zemon. *Society and Culture in Early Modern France: Eight Essays*. Stanford: Stanford University Press, 1975.

_____. "Some Tasks and Themes in the Study of Popular Religion," in *The Pursuit of Holiness*, eds. Charles Trinkhaus and Heiko Oberman. Leiden: Brill, 1974.

de Beauvoir, Simone. *The Second Sex*, trans. and ed. H. M. Parshley. New York: Bantam Books, 1952.

Delaruelle, E., et al. *L'Église au temps du Grand Schisme et de la crise conciliare, 1378-1449*. Paris: Bloud et Gay, 1964.

Delcambre, E. *Le Concept de la Sorcellerie dans le Duché de Lorraine*. Nancy, 1948-51. 3 vols.

Delumeau, Jean. *Le Catholicisme entre Luther et Voltaire*. Paris: Nouvelle Clio, 1971.

Douglas, Mary. *Witchcraft: Confessions and Accusations*. London, 1970.

Duby, George. *Rural Economy and Country Life in the Medieval West*. trans. C. Postan. Paris, 1962. Columbia: University of South Carolina Press, 1968.

Edelman, Nathan. *Attitudes of Seventeenth-Century France toward the Middle Ages*. New York: Columbia University Press, 1946.

Eliade, Mircea. *Shamanism: Archaic Techniques of Ecstasy*. Trans. W. R. Trask. Paris, 1951. Princeton: Bollingen Foundation/Princeton University Press, 1964.

Finucane, Ronald C. *Miracles and Pilgrims: Popular Beliefs in Medieval England*. Totowa, N. J.: Rowman and Littlefield, 1977.

Geary, Patrick J. "The Ninth-Century Relic Trade: a Response to Popular Piety?" in *Religion and the People*, ed. J. Obelkevich. Chapel Hill: University of North Carolina Press, 1978.

Gies, Frances, and Joseph Gies. *Women in the Middle Ages.* New York: Barnes and Noble, 1978.

Grundmann, Herbert. *Religiöse Bewegungen im Mittelalter,* 2nd ed. Hildesheim, 1961.

Happold, F. C. *Mysticism.* Baltimore: Penguin Books, 1970.

Hay, Denys. *Europe in the Fourteenth and Fifteenth Centuries.* New York: Holt, Rinehart and Winston, 1966.

Heilbrun, Carolyn. *Towards a Recognition of Androgyny.* New York: Alfred A. Knopf, 1973.

Herm, Gerhard. *The Celts: The People Who Came Out of the Darkness.* New York: St. Martin's Press, 1976.

Holmes, George. *Europe: Hierarchy and Revolt: 1320-1480.* London: Wm. Collins and Sons, 1975.

_____. "Cardinal Beaufort and the Crusade against the Hussites," in *English Historical Review* 42 (October, 1973): 721-50.

Holdsworth, C. J. "Christina of Markyate," *Medieval Women,* ed. Derek Baker (Oxford: Ecclesiastical History Society, 1978), 185-204.

Jacquin, R. "Un précurseur de Jeanne d'Arc." *Revue des Deux Mondes,* May 15, 1967: 222-26.

Kelly, Joan. "Early Feminist Theory and the 'Querelle des Femmes,' 1400-1789," in *Signs: Journal of Women in Culture and Society* 8.1 (Autumn, 1982): 4-28.

Kieckhefer, Richard. "Radical Tendencies in the Flagellant Movement of the Mid-Fourteenth Century." JMRS 4 (1977): 157-76.

_____. *European Witch Trials: Their Foundations in Popular and Learned Culture, 1300-1500.* Berkeley: University of California Press, 1976.

_____. *The Repression of Heresy in Germany.* Philadelphia: University of Pennsylvania Press, 1979.

Lambert, Malcolm. *Medieval Heresy: Popular Movements from Bogamil to Hus.* New York, 1977.

Lang, Andrew. *Miracles of St. Katherine of Fierbois.* Chicago: Nutt, 1897.

Lea, Henry C. *A History of the Inquisition of the Middle Ages,* vols. II and III. New York: Harper & Row, 1888.

Lefkowitz, Mary. *Heroines and Hysterics.* New York: St. Martin's Press, 1981.

Lerner, Robert. *The Heresy of the Free Spirit in the Late Middle Ages.* Berkeley: University of California Press, 1972.

Lewis, I. M. *Ecstatic Religion: An Anthropological Study of Spirit Possession and Shamanism.* Baltimore: Penguin Books, 1971.

Macfarlane, Alan. *Witchcraft in Tudor and Stuart England.* New York: Harper & Row, 1970.

May, William H. "The Confession of Prous Boneta, Heretic and Heresiarch," in *Essays in Medieval Life and Thought.* New York: Columbia University Press, 1955.

McDonnell, Ernest. *Beguines and Beghards in Medieval Culture.* 1954. New York: Octagon Books, 1969.

McLaughlin, Eleanor. "The Heresy of the Free Spirit and Late Medieval Mysticism." *Medievalia et Humanistica* n.s.4 (1973).

Metraux, Alfred. *Voodoo in Haiti,* trans. Hugo Charteris. New York: Schocken Books, 1972.

Muchembled, Robert. "The Witches of the Cambrésis: The Acculturation of the Rural World in the Sixteenth and Seventeenth Centuries." In *Religion and the People, 800-1700,* ed. J. Obelkevich. Chapel Hill: University of North Carolina Press, 1978.

————. "Witchcraft, Popular Culture, and Christianity in the Sixteenth Century." In *Ritual, Religion, and the Sacred,* ed. R. Forster and O. Ranum, 213-36. Baltimore: Johns Hopkins University Press, 1982.

Murray, Alexander. *Reason and Society in the Middle Ages.* Oxford: Claredon Press, 1978.

Nochlin, Linda. "Iconography versus Ideology: Power and Powerlessness in Nineteenth-Century Images of Women." Unpublished paper, forthcoiming.

Obelkevich, James, ed.. *Religion and the People: 800-1700.* Chapel Hill: University of North Carolina Press 1978.

O'Brien, Elmer. *Varieties of Mystic Experience.* London: Mentor-Omega Books, 1973.

O'Brien, John A. *The Inquisition.* New York: Macmillan, 1973.

Ozment, Steven. *Mysticism and Dissent: Religious Ideology and Social Protest in the Sixteenth Century*. New Haven: Yale University Press, 1973.

————. *The Age of Reform: 1250-1550*. New Haven: Yale University Press, 1980.

Parrinder, Geoffrey. *West African Religion*, 2nd ed. New York: Barnes & Noble, 1961.

Peters, Edward. *The Magician, the Witch, and the Law*. Philadelphia: University of Pennsylvania Press, 1978.

Poliakov, Leon. *The History of Antisemitism*, trans. Richard Howard. New York: Schocken Books, 1974.

Redfield, Robert. *Peasant Society and Culture: An Anthropological Approach to Civilization*. Chicago: University of Chicago Press, 1977.

Reeves, Marjorie. *Joachim of Fiore and the Prophetic Future*. New York: Harper & Row, 1977.

Riehle, Wolfgang. *Studien zur englischen Mystik des Mittelalters*. Heidelberg, 1977.

Rike, Mrs. D. L. "Memorial Address" to the General Conference of the United Brethren in Christ, 1877, in *Faith That Achieved: A History of the Women's Missionary Association of the Church of the United Brethren in Christ, 1872-1946*, by Mary R. Hough. Dayton, Ohio, 1958.

Rousselle, Aline. "From Sanctuary to Miracle-Worker: Healing in Fourth-Century Gaul," in *Ritual, Religion, and the Sacred*, eds. R. Forster and O. Ranum. Baltimore: Johns Hopkins University Press, 1982.

Russell, Jeffrey B. *Dissent and Reform in the Early Middle Ages*. Berkeley: University of California Press, 1965.

————. *Witchcraft in the Middle Ages*. Secaucus: Citadel Press, 1972.

Solle, Dorothee. "A Feminist Reflection: Mysticism, Liberation and the Name of God." *Christianity and Crisis* 41, no. 11 (June 22, 1981): 179-85.

Southern, R. W. *The Making of the Middle Ages*. London: Penguin Books, 1973.

Tavard, George H. *Woman in Christian Tradition*. South Bend: University of Notre Dame Press, 1973.

Thomas, Keith. *Religion and the Decline of Magic*. New York: Scribners, 1971.

Thomsen, Harry. *The New Religions of Japan*. Tokyo: Charles E. Tuttle Co., 1963.

Thomson, John A. F. *The Later Lollards, 1414-1520*. Oxford: Oxford University Press, 1965.

Toussaert, Jacques. *Le sentiment religieux en Flandre à la fin du moyen âge*. Paris: Plon, 1963.

Trinkhaus, Charles, and Heiko Oberman, eds. *The Pursuit of Holiness in the Late Middle Ages and Renaissance*. Leiden: Brill, 1974.

Vale, Malcolm. *Charles VII*. Berkeley: University of California Press, 1974.

Vaughan, Richard. *John the Fearless: The Growth of Burgundian Power*. London: Longman, 1966, 1977.

————. *Philip the Good*. London: Longman, 1970.

Ward, Benedicta. *Miracles and the Medieval Mind: Theory, Record, and Event, 1000-1215*. Philadelphia: University of Pennsylvania Press, 1982.

Wentz, Evans W. Y. *The Fairy-Faith in Celtic Countries*. Oxford, 1911; Gerrards Cross: Colin Smythe Ltd., 1977.

Wessley, Stephen E. "The Thirteenth-Century Guglielmites: Salvation Through Women," in Derek Baker, ed. *Medieval Women*, q. v.

Wilson, Bryan. *The Noble Savages: the Primitive Origins of Charisma and its Contemporary Survival*. London, 1975.

Woods, Richard, ed. *Understanding Mysticism*. Garden City: Doubleday and Co., 1980.

Index

STUDIES IN WOMEN AND RELIGION